DYING FOR ANSWERS

Expendable Workers of the Cold War Nuclear Testing

DOT CLAYTON

Copyright © 2016 Dot Clayton.

All rights reserved. No part of this book may be used or reproduced by any means, graphic, electronic, or mechanical, including photocopying, recording, taping or by any information storage retrieval system without the written permission of the author except in the case of brief quotations embodied in critical articles and reviews.

LifeRich Publishing is a registered trademark of The Reader's Digest Association, Inc.

LifeRich Publishing books may be ordered through booksellers or by contacting:

LifeRich Publishing
1663 Liberty Drive
Bloomington, IN 47403
www.liferichpublishing.com
1 (888) 238-8637

Because of the dynamic nature of the Internet, any web addresses or links contained in this book may have changed since publication and may no longer be valid. The views expressed in this work are solely those of the author and do not necessarily reflect the views of the publisher, and the publisher hereby disclaims any responsibility for them.

Any people depicted in stock imagery provided by Thinkstock are models, and such images are being used for illustrative purposes only.
Certain stock imagery © Thinkstock.

ISBN: 978-1-4897-1052-9 (sc)
ISBN: 978-1-4897-1053-6 (e)

Print information available on the last page.

LifeRich Publishing rev. date: 04/12/2017

PREFACE

This book tells a true story that details a gripping account and shares the critical decisions made by all agencies involved in the Cold War underground nuclear bomb testing. Because men are not angels, government is necessary. However, our government seemed to have "gone their own way" long before we could have ever imagined. Those in control of protecting our country also have a moral obligation to protect the workers and citizens of our great country. This book is dedicated to the brave men and women involved in the testing of nuclear bombs during our Cold War with Russia. They faced an enemy they could not see, could not destroy, and would not go away … ever!

This Book is dedicated to
Glenn Aaron Clayton
And all the victims of the
Cold War.

Chapter I

DE-CLASSIFIED RECORDS REVEALED

This is a true story about the Nevada Test Site (NTS), government cover-ups, denials, and disinformation by the Atomic Energy Commission (AEC), later known as Department of Energy (DOE), Reynolds Electrical and Engineering Co., Inc. (REECo), and other related groups during the Cold War nuclear testing program. It's the story of one man's courage and dedication to his country and his employer. It's about his personal contributions to the nuclear weapons testing program and its role in keeping the United States of America a world superpower. The information shared here regards radiation exposure to the employees at the NTS, and it was obtained from 1,370 pages of previously classified employment records on one NTS employee named Glenn Aaron Clayton. After months of refusal by the Department of Energy, these records were finally released on June 5, 2000, through the Freedom of Information Act—exactly one year to the day after his death. The records specifically cover the excessive deadly radiation exposure Glenn received from 1958 through 1970. They cover in detail Glenn's involvement in the underground testing of nuclear bombs detonated specifically in the NTS Area 12 tunnels during the Cold War.

My name is Dorothy Clayton, Glenn's wife of more than twenty-five years. I wanted to share these previously classified government records in my possession because I believe it is a story that needs to be told. I was employed at the NTS from July 1962 to February 1978 by Holmes and Narver Engineering Company (H&N). H&N was a subcontractor responsible for many types of support jobs relating to nuclear testing at the NTS.

After Glenn's death on June 5, 1999, I was very curious to see his radiation exposure history, and I requested a copy of his employment records from REECo because I believed Glenn's seven different types of deadly cancers was caused by excessive radiation exposure. REECo sent me to DOE because they were "in charge" of all employee records of employment. My request was denied, and I was informed by the DOE that Glenn's employment records were classified government property, and would not be released to anyone. It was hard to believe that employment records could be labeled "classified government property."

Not long after my request to the DOE had been refused, I happened to see an article in the *Las Vegas Review Journal* newspaper, stating,

> The Department of Energy is having an open meeting on Monday at the DOE building in Las Vegas, and would like to hear from anyone with a family member, previously employed at the NTS, who presently has cancer, or who has died from cancer. Everyone will have 5 minutes to speak to the Asst. Secretary of Energy, Dr. David Michaels and Senator Reid's representative from Washington.

Immediately, I began preparing a five-minute speech for the Monday morning meeting. I arrived early at the DOE building, and the meeting room was close to being filled. Many people were standing in the hallway where they could look through a plate glass window into the meeting room. Loudspeakers were in place to broadcast everything to the people standing in the hallway. On a table near the door of the meeting room was a list of people who wanted to speak. I was number twenty-seven on the list.

I spotted an empty chair close to the front of the room and hurriedly made my way to the front. When it came time for me to speak, I got their attention when I told them about Glenn's seven different types of cancers. And I mentioned that I had been denied access by the DOE to Glenn's employment records. When the five minutes were over, a bell sounded, letting me know my time was up, so I thanked them for being there, and I went back to my chair. Senator Reid's representative from his Washington, DC, office, immediately came over to where I was sitting, gave me his business card, and asked me to call him the next day. I made the call and spoke with the Washington representative. He was especially concerned that I was denied access to Glenn's employment records. He assured me that he would help with getting those records released.

Chapter II

THE PRESS CONFERENCE

Two days later I got approval from the Department of Energy to pick up all of Glenn's previously classified employment records from the DOE office in Las Vegas.

Upon arrival at the DOE office, I was met by an employee who made it obvious I was not welcome there. She pointed to a Xerox box sitting on a table and informed me that if I wanted anything else, I would be charged twenty-five cents per page. I took the box and left. When I got home and opened the box, what a shock! There were 1,370 pages of very important government employment documents that had been *thrown* into a Xerox box. They weren't in any type of order—by year, radiation exposure, tests for contamination, etc. It was in total disarray.

Right away my instinct told me that someone had deliberately arranged those records in that order to confuse anyone trying to make sense out of them. That's when I was very thankful I had the knowledge and experience from years of NTS employment to put those records in the proper order by dates, nuclear tests, and results. It took exactly two weeks for me to get that job done. But when I did get the 1,370 pages arranged in order, those records told a very sad and heartbreaking story of cover-up and betrayal of a dedicated and loyal employee of REECo for almost thirty years. I began to see exactly what had been *purposely* done to Glenn with the approval of the AEC, DOE, and REECo.

It was shocking to see such blatant disregard to human life, which was evident on almost every nuclear event that Glenn was involved in. I could then see why they had chosen to hide these employee records under the label "classified and confidential."

Immediately, I contacted Senator Reid's regional manager and let him know what was in the box of Glenn's employment records that the DOE had given me. The regional manager arranged a press conference with Senator Reid in my Las Vegas home on May 31, 2000. I was overwhelmed when four TV channel reporters with cameramen, two newspaper reporters, the DOE manager, Senator Reid, and his staff from the Las Vegas office and his DC office all showed up at my door. It was standing room only in my living room, kitchen, dining room, and hallway!

After that press conference, I was invited to Washington, DC, to tell Glenn's story to several senators. Our Nevada Senator's regional manager set up appointments for meetings the following week. I packed a bag and left the next morning for Washington, DC.

Those five days of meetings turned out to be very beneficial. There were several other DOE facilities performing different but just as deadly nuclear testing experiments, such as Oak Ridge, Tennessee, and Hanford, Washington, and their senators were unaware of the government cover-ups regarding excessive radiation exposure to employees in their states. All of the senators and representatives I spoke with were thankful for the information.

Chapter III

DOE RECORDS EVALUATED

The Advisory Board on Radiation and Worker Health (ABRWH) was established to maintain openness in its deliberations regarding NTS worker employment records and radiation exposure. The ABRWH hired S. Cohen & Associates (SC&A) of Vienna, Virginia, to interview me and evaluate the records I had gotten from the DOE. Here is their summary of that four-hour interview.

> Ms. Clayton raised several issues regarding potential inconsistencies between the Film Badge Cards and other records. The Film Badge Cards are particularly difficult to read. In many cases, they do not contain printed dose information and must be read by a computer program to obtain a value. Where they did include dose information, in many cases, the result is not printed under the correct column. For example, in many cases the batch number is printed in the column labeled *"mrem this year." In other cases, Film Badge Cards provide densitometer readings in blocks labeled "Dosage Reading."
>
> > *Mrem—quantities measured in mrem are designed to represent biological effects of ionizing radiation primarily radiation-induced cancer.

A concern raised several times by Ms. Clayton was the overexposure to her husband to radiation. She also indicated there was pressure to not wear dosimeters. Experienced miners were so critical that memorandum and investigation report in Mr. Clayton's dosimetry file indicate that as many as 30 miners were approaching the legal dose limits in 1961. The AEC was approached to raise the allowed limit from 5R to 12R per year. In a letter from Maupin (NTS) to Tyler (AEC). Maupin (1961) said, "The present criteria are unrealistic for operational period and not in keeping with the intent of a weapon development program having to do with the defense capability of the Country."

In the investigation report, a Radiological Safety Division employee was told by the mine superintendent that he "could not jeopardize the schedule for insignificant exposures." That same superintendent therefore permitted the workers to enter the tunnel. Because of the desire to meet schedules and the lack of skilled miners, these workers were exposed to doses approaching or exceeding the limits as established by the AEC.

In summary, with so many sources of internal and external information it can become confusing, for even a health physicist, to navigate the dosimetry records. The constituents of whole body dose are often not clearly defined. This difficulty is compounded by the large volume of records provided for some claimants, (e.g., greater than 1000 pages). Mr. Clayton's files indicate that the practice of sampling individuals with positive nasal smears was not consistently applied. In some cases, there was potential for alpha exposure without corresponding bioassay sampling.

A few months after I returned to Las Vegas from the Washington, DC, trip, I moved to Tennessee. A short time after my move to Tennessee, I received a phone call from one of the TV reporters who had been at the press conference in my home in Las Vegas. He wanted to bring his cameraman to Tennessee and do a lengthy interview and take photos of some of Glenn's records. The reporter called one of the memos "the smoking gun." He was referring to one of the memo from the radiation safety chief to REECo manager that said, "Remove Mr. Clayton from his present job and place him in another job where his radiation exposure would be eliminated entirely." However, that recommendation in 1958 was ignored, and Glenn spent another twelve years working in that deadly environment.

The reporter and his cameraman did a great job, and they were given eight minutes on the 5:00 p.m. news in Las Vegas (channel 13) to tell Glenn's story. The story also made the front page (top half) of the Las Vegas newspaper. Finally, the "curtain of secrecy" was pulled back, and the AEC, DOE, REECo, and others involved in the cover-up were exposed.

I began writing this story in 2000, but because it was painful at that time, I put everything away. Enough time has passed now that I am ready to tackle the job.

We now know that the biggest losers of the Cold War were the dedicated, hardworking men in the nuclear weapons testing program. The majority of those workers were WWII veterans stepping up once again to do whatever was necessary to protect their country. They had no idea that job would eventually—and prematurely—take their lives.

Chapter IV

BEGINNING OF THE COLD WAR

The Cold War was a state of political and military tension after WWII between powers in the Western Bloc (the United States, its NATO allies, and others) and powers in the Eastern Bloc (the Soviet Union and its satellite states).

During World War II, the United States and the Soviet Union fought together as allies against the Axis powers. However, the relationship between the two nations was always very tense. The United States had long been wary of Soviet communism and concerned about Russian leader Joseph Stalin's seemingly bloodthirsty rule over his own country. The Soviets resented the Americans' decades-long refusal to treat the USSR as a part of the international community.

The term *cold* was used because there was no large-scale fighting directly between the two sides, although there were major regional wars, known as "proxy wars," supported by the two sides. The Cold War split the temporary wartime alliance against Nazi Germany, leaving the Soviet Union and the United States as two superpowers with profound economic and political differences. The USSR was a Marxist-Leninist state ruled by its Communist Party and the secret police, who in turn were ruled by a dictator (Stalin) or a small committee (politburo). The party controlled the press, the military, the economy, and all organizations. It also controlled the states in the Eastern Bloc and funded Communist parties around the world.

In opposition stood the West, dominantly democratic and capitalist with a free press and independent organizations. A small neutral bloc arose with the Non-Aligned Movement and sought good relations with both sides. The two superpowers never engaged directly in full-scale armed combat. But they were both heavily armed in preparation for a possible all-out nuclear world war. Each side had a nuclear armament that deterred an attack by the other side on the basis that such an attack would lead to total destruction of the attacker—the doctrine of mutually assured destruction (MAD).

The Cold War years left a significant legacy. It is often referred to in movies with themes of espionage, especially in the internationally successful James Bond movies, the threat of nuclear warfare.

Several years prior to Glenn's employment at the NTS, the Manhattan Project was formed in September 1942 to secretly build an atomic bomb—certainly before the Germans had a chance to build one. The army appointed General Leslie Groves to head the effort. Los Alamos, New Mexico, was selected in November of that year as the site for an atomic bomb laboratory. The top secret laboratory was built deep within the mountains of New Mexico. The scientists were only told they would be working on a project that might end the war. The army built numerous temporary buildings to house the scientists and their families, who for security reasons could not leave Los Alamos except in case of a dire emergency. Nearly five thousand people lived and worked at Los Alamos at the close of the war.

The Manhattan Project built a top secret complex of nuclear production and research facilities across the country, employing three hundred thousand workers. Secrecy was so complete that the hundreds of thousands of workers didn't know what they were working on until they heard about the bombing of Hiroshima, Japan.

An atomic bomb code-named Trinity was ready to be tested on July 16, 1945, and an area just outside Alamogordo, New Mexico, was selected as the site for the detonation.

Trinity was a spectacular success. A big black circle burned on the ground there still marks the desert floor where the first atmospheric test of an atomic bomb was conducted. That testing area became what we know today as "White Sands Missile Range," and that first explosion paved the way for the go-ahead to bomb Hiroshima and Nagasaki, Japan, only weeks later. It also was the precursor to many hundreds of nuclear test detonations by the United States. The early postwar tests were done in the atmosphere at Bikini Atoll and Eniwetok Atoll in the Pacific and at the Nevada Proving Grounds, which was later renamed the "Nevada Test Site."

Historians have speculated that President Truman felt it was a necessity to move most of the nation's nuclear testing from the Pacific, where it had been accomplished in the early atomic testing program, to an interior location where it might be less observable and where troops could protect the project from potential wartime attack and sabotage. President Truman put together a special panel of the National Security Council whose task was to select the most appropriate location to accommodate the testing program. In combination with advisors, Truman chose a location in Nye County, Nevada, which at that time was one of the largest bombing gunnery ranges for the US Air Force. The area was dubbed "the Nevada Test Site" (not terribly inventive but surely descriptive) on December 31, 1954.

Chapter V

ARRIVING AT SCHOFIELD BARRACKS

Glenn's involvement in nuclear bomb detonations dates back to the first atomic bomb. Upon enlistment in the US Army-Air Force on October 5, 1943, he was trained in chemical warfare and first aid. He was first sent to Honolulu, Hawaii, to serve with the 88th Airdrome Squadron. Upon arrival in Honolulu, he and several other soldiers were picked up at the airfield, herded into the bed of a large army truck, and told they were being taken to Schofield Barracks. As the truck approached the US Army-Air Force facility, all the men saw were rows and rows of tents. The only barracks to be found at Schofield Barracks, were officer's quarters.

After being assigned to their two-man tents and getting settled in, the new arrivals went out to meet the other soldiers. It wasn't long before the new arrivals decided that being in a tent in Hawaii did have its benefits. Several times a week, a small group of the young soldiers would slip out of camp after dark and slowly make their way across the pineapple fields to the bars in Honolulu. They would party as long as possible, and sometimes make it back to their tents just before sunrise. They would make reveille and get through their assigned duties for the day. And after a good night's sleep, they were ready to sneak back into Honolulu the next night.

Then on January 15, 1945, Glenn was transferred to the island of Tinian, located in the Northern Mariana Islands, to serve with the 87th Airdrome Squadron. When Sergeant Clayton and his nicely tanned crew arrived on Tinian, they noticed, among other things, an oversized hangar being constructed at what was known as "North Field." The soldiers were curious but were told, "Do not ask questions, and do not go near that hangar!" These obedient soldiers knew the slogan "Loose lips sink ships" and didn't ask questions ... or go near the hangar. They surely never thought that huge hangar would soon house a specially modified B-29 bomber that would carry an atomic bomb!

This new duty station certainly was nothing like the lush island of Oahu, Hawaii, these soldiers had just left. Tinian Island was full of nothing but coconut trees and a gray sandy beach that was not very inviting. But with a lot of spare time and imagination and with only coconut trees and a dry sandy beach, these dedicated soldiers decided to make the best of the situation.

They gathered coconuts and learned how to make coconut beer. They found some jars, broke open several coconuts, and poured the coconut milk into the jars. Then after covering the jars with someone's tee shirt, they let the jars sit until the "smell" was just right. These creative soldiers then tied strings around the jars and carefully set them in the ocean to cool. They designated Friday night as party night to try their own coconut "original island beer" recipe. Needless to say, when Saturday morning came, some of the soldiers did have to report to sick bay!

The young soldiers got updates every day on the war, and in April 1945, they learned that US troops had liberated the Nazi concentration camp at Buchenwald. Then in May 1945, Germany surrendered, and that was cause for a special "coconut beer" party. And the next morning a line of brave soldiers reported to sick bay one more time!

Chapter VI

MODIFIED B-29 BOMBER

One thing these young soldiers didn't know—and could never have imagined—was that during this time the United States was busy building an atomic bomb. A B-29 bomber was being modified specifically for the highly secret atomic bomb mission. It was outfitted with a new engine and propellers and faster-acting pneumatic bay doors for the bomb. The B-29 was manufactured by the Glenn L. Martin Aircraft Company in Omaha, Nebraska. The plane carried the atomic bomb from Wendover Army-Air Force Base in Utah to Guam, where the modifications for the bomb bay doors were completed. Then it was carried by US Navy cruiser *Indianapolis* from Guam and arrived at Tinian Island on July 12, 1945.

The atomic bomb, code-named "Little Boy," was nine feet long and weighed four tons. During July, the B-29 bomber made eight practice (training) flights and flew two missions on July 24 and 26 to drop pumpkins on industrial targets at Kobe and Nagoya, Japan. On July 31, 1945, the *Enola Gay* (named the *Enola Gay* after pilot Paul Tibbits's mother) was used on a rehearsal flight for the actual mission.

On August 6, 1945, just twenty days before Glenn's twenty-first birthday, the B-29 bomber took off from North Field in Tinian Island. Colonel Paul Tibbits knew, but for security purposes, the crew was not informed of the reason for the *Enola Gay's* early morning mission until after takeoff. The *Enola Gay* mission was to "drop the atomic bomb on Hiroshima, Japan."

At 7:25 a.m., the Enola Gay was cruising close to Hiroshima. At 8:00 a.m., the Japanese detected the bomber heading toward Hiroshima. The radio station quickly broadcast a warning for the people to take shelter, but many did not follow this advice.

At 8:09 a.m., the *Enola Gay's* crew could see the city appear below. It was almost time to drop the bomb. Just then the crew received a message indicating that the weather was good over Hiroshima.

At 8:15 a.m. (Hiroshima local time) on August 6, 1945, the atomic bomb was released over Hiroshima. It was the first atomic bomb used in war.

With the mission completed, Colonel Paul Tibbits made a sharp U-turn and headed the *Enola Gay* back to Tinian Island. On the turn the crew got a good look at the huge mushroom cloud coming up from the drop zone. They were shocked, afraid, amazed, and certainly very happy that their mission was over and successful. The entire crew was extremely relieved when the *Enola Gay* arrived back on Tinian Island exactly twelve hours and thirteen minutes after takeoff.

On the return flight, Col. Tibbits summed up the changes in his time in the following quote:

> Now on the return flight, I reflected on the wonders of science and rejoiced that the new weapon had surely made future war unthinkable. Just as the spear had been more deadly than the club, the bow and arrow a more formidable weapon than the spear, gunpowder had made the bow and arrow obsolete. Each technological advance in weaponry had made war more hideous, but so far had not persuaded mankind to abandon this means of settling quarrels between peoples. Now certainly we had developed the ultimate argument for keeping the peace.

On August 9, 1945, another atomic bomb was dropped on the city of Nagasaki, Japan. Those bombs were dropped to end a war of massive death and destruction, and it worked. A few days later, the war ended when Japan surrendered, four years after they had bombed Pearl Harbor.

Japan officially surrendered on September 2, 1945, aboard the battleship *USS Missouri* in Tokyo Bay. It was highly unlikely that Japan would have unconditionally surrendered without such an invasion.

When Hiroshima was bombed, the bomb appeared as a promise of peace to the entire world. It ended a costly and gruesome war, beginning a time of peace. Compared to the technology of 1945, the atomic bomb looked too powerful and unethical ever to be used again. It was seen as the weapon that would put an end to the war. However, with a bomb so powerful that it could destroy humanity, people began to realize what their potential was. Man could split an atom! Man now had the confidence to master new technological discoveries. Aside from the advances in science and medicine came the advances in weaponry, a deadly growth in man's upward trend.

How in the world did a small group of people, transplanted to a tiny isolated community deep in the mountains of northern New Mexico, conceive of a weapon that would forever change history?

Chapter VII

NUCLEAR AGE BECOMES A REALITY

The nuclear age became a reality! Glenn's involvement in nuclear bomb explosions dates back to the first atomic bomb used in war. But he had no idea he would spend the majority of the rest of his life right in the middle of it.

After the war ended and Glenn was honorably discharged from the US Army-Air Force in 1946, he returned home to Salt Lake City, Utah. He was born and raised in Salt Lake City. He had attended school in SLC and had played on the Beet Diggers football team. When he joined the Army-Air Force, he followed his three older brothers to fight for his country. The oldest brother was one of the soldiers involved in the Normandy invasion and was on one of the boats that landed on Omaha Beach.

Once back home Glenn began a career in mining. Then in June 1958, while working at a Kennecott copper mine just outside Ruth, Nevada, he received a phone call from a friend telling him that miners were badly needed at the Nevada Test Site (NTS). He was told that the job paid extremely well and would last three months. He drove to Las Vegas, applied for the job, and went to work immediately for Reynolds Electrical and Engineering Co., Inc. (REECo). That three-month job lasted almost thirty years!

REECo was advertising for miners in 1958 because this was the very beginning of testing nuclear bombs in tunnels. This required the skills and expertise of underground miners. Previously all underground *shots* occurred in deep holes bored into the earth. So Glenn was *in* right at the beginning of the *new* underground testing program.

Inside the tunnels was an assembly area where small railroad cars would carry men and equipment deeper into the tunnel, which had been bored into the side of one of the mountains in Area 12. Average assembly area in the tunnels averaged 33 feet wide by 38 feet high by 176 feet long. Many nuclear tests could be detonated in separate holes drilled into the side of the each tunnel. Much of the time after a nuclear detonation, a part of the tunnel would be so contaminated with deadly radiation that it could not be rehabilitated, and it would become necessary to seal that area off permanently.

Chapter VIII

THE NEVADA TEST SITE WAS BORN

The NTS main gate was located sixty-five miles north of Las Vegas, Nevada, on Highway 95. The actual nuclear testing at that time was conducted in tunnels several miles east of the main gate, specifically known as Area 12. The Nevada desert was chosen by members of Congress and approved by the president to detonate nuclear bombs. Our government approved the use of 1,375 square miles for the test site. An additional adjacent several hundred miles were set aside for future use.

Included in the Nevada Test Site is Yucca Mountain, where nuclear waste is stored. This area also includes Area 51, still the most secret government facility in the United States. The Desert Rock landing strip is located a short distance north of the NTS main gate with another landing strip located in Area 12 on Pahute Mesa. There were also ten heliports spread throughout the NTS.

Some employees who worked in Mercury rather than staying at the NTS chose to ride back and forth on a daily basis aboard the many sixty-two-passenger buses provided by our government. They were picked up at certain pickup points in Las Vegas for the ride to and from the test site. On the one hour bus ride each way, the workers usually took the opportunity to catch up on some sleep or hone their card-playing skills in anticipation of their next trip to the Las Vegas casinos. Entry into the Nevada Test Site was difficult. As you approached the NTS main gate, you were met by two very stern-looking armed security guards.

All employees were required to have complete background checks before they were issued a "Q" clearance security badge that gave them access into the NTS. The security guards actually touched the badge, making sure the badge was authentic and issued by the Atomic Energy Commission. The guards had their own secret way of making sure the badge was authentic. If you happened to be a passenger on one of the busses—and heaven forbid if you happened to be asleep when the bus arrived at the main gate—the guards gave a "not so gentle" shove, waking you in a flash. You immediately knew to hold your badge so the guard could physically *touch* it.

After you were given permission by the guards to enter the NTS and they waved the bus on through the gate, you entered what resembled "small town America." This would be the government town of Mercury, Nevada. There, you would see many small buildings that housed subcontractor offices as well as a medical facility staffed with a medical doctor and nurses. One of the buildings was home of the very best steak house and cafeteria in Nevada.

Entering the NTS, you would also see a fire station, the sheriff's substation, a post office, and a large motor pool with an automotive repair shop. One of the buildings housed a first-class bowling alley. There was also an Olympic size swimming pool that you could not see from the main road. A group of trailers for workers who wanted to stay at the NTS all week was located on the north side of those buildings. These trailers had a bedroom on each end and a bathroom in the middle. The trailers could house two single men or a married couple *if* they were both employed by one of the NTS contractors.

The AEC wanted to make absolutely sure nothing was left out for the comfort and convenience of the NTS employees working in this small government town. Money was no object. So for the after-work entertainment, the men employees living in their trailers formed baseball teams. The women living in their trailers became the cheerleaders for the baseball team! For their pleasure and entertainment, there were also mixed bowling leagues and swimming teams for "fun and games" after work.

Just outside the NTS main gate was a Department of Motor Vehicles Office, where employees could renew their personal vehicles license plates. Everything an employee needed was right there in Mercury.

Chapter IX

SMALL TOWN LAS VEGAS

In the 1940s and 50s, Las Vegas was just a small gambling town. But the town enjoyed a military boom as WWII bases gave way to Cold War facilities, most famously, the Nevada Test Site, where more than a hundred nuclear bombs were detonated. Between 1951 and 1963, mushroom clouds were often visible from the hotels in Las Vegas. Postcards proclaimed, "Las Vegas the 'Up and Atom' City."

The NTS employees donated their fair share of money to the Las Vegas boom. Desperate for the challenge to take away some of the casino money, many workers headed toward the casinos whenever the chance arose. Some of the men would gamble their entire paycheck on one roll of the dice. More times than not, they would lose an entire week's pay and then drive back to the NTS, work another week, and do a repeat on their next trip to Las Vegas.

This compulsive addiction to gambling became hazardous to a lot of marriages. Many of the wives of those NTS workers would be in the casinos on a daily basis, playing the slot machines and losing their husbands entire paychecks on that addiction. That problem alone caused many of the workers to pack up and move their families back to their hometowns.

REECo was the main contractor and responsible for hiring the majority of employees for the NTS. All of the union workers were available through the union offices in Las Vegas. Finding office workers was not a problem. Those jobs were filled fast. But the maintenance worker jobs were not easily filled. Someone in REECo came up with the idea of driving several sixty-two-passenger buses from Las Vegas to Tallulah, Louisiana, in search of prospective employees to fill these jobs, and that endeavor was successful.

They brought back almost the entire town, mostly black men and women, and they became a great workforce for the NTS. Coming from that small town of less than three thousand residents, never before in their young lives did it occur to these residents of Tallulah the amount of money the government would pay for sweeping floors, digging ditches, and cleaning bathrooms! A dream—never realized—came true.

From 1958 through 1970, Glenn's declassified work records detail his work in Area 12, driving tunnels, making tunnel reentries after detonations, and directing workers in preparations of and clean up after a nuclear detonation. His job classifications included miner, shift boss, general foreman, assistant superintendent, superintendent, and project manager.

In 1958, the Nevada Test Site went on a twenty-four-hour, seven-day workweek because the Cold War was escalating and the United States needed to rapidly test new weapon design strategies against a possible nuclear war with Russia. At that time all nuclear bomb detonations were done in Area 12. The nuclear tests were conducted in several different tunnel locations on Rainier Mesa. A horizontal line of sight (HLOS) pipe was used in preparation for the nuclear blast. This was done for radiation effects research. A large tunnel complex mined under the mesa would contain the HLOS pipe.

The HLOS pipe is 1,500 to 1,800 feet long and tapers from eight to ten inches up to thirty feet in diameter at the detonation chamber, where a nuclear bomb is placed several inches from the working point. At zero time the nuclear bomb is fired, and instantaneously, radiation would flow down the pipe. However, there was always containment problems with keeping the radiation in the pipes because the pipes would often crack when the nuclear detonation occurred. Deadly radiation was always escaping into the tunnel areas, contaminating the workers.

Cameras were placed in the tunnel area to capture the explosion. The scientists and managers watched the detonation from a control point (CP) several miles away. They could visually observe the desert floor heaving, resembling a two-foot or higher ocean wave heading toward the CP building. Of course, the building had been specially designed and constructed to withstand that kind of shock wave.

After the nuclear detonation, radiation safety monitors would check radiation content and type in the detonation area. When radiation readings were supposedly at a safe level, the reentry team would be sent back into the tunnel to recover what was left of the instruments used in the nuclear detonation. What was left of the instruments enabled the scientists to gather valuable information relating to the type of explosion and results from the nuclear bomb detonation. Workers would then be sent back into the tunnel to rehabilitate the area and make it ready for another nuclear bomb test as soon as possible.

Since the nuclear testing program was new, there were no formal radiation exposure guidelines. However, there has been some knowledge about radiation exposure gained since the bombing of Hiroshima and Nagasaki. They knew that excessive amounts of radiation were always present and deadly after a nuclear bomb detonation.

No one knew *how much* "excessive radiation exposure" was deadly. And so the workers kept on being sent into hazardous areas with the main focus being to "get the job done and win the Cold War!" Later on, everyone knew the heavy price paid for that dedication and commitment of the men working in those tunnels. That news was overwhelming!

Chapter X

DEADLY RADIATION EXPOSURE

On October 13, 1959, the radiation safety chief wrote a memo to AEC that read,

> The following is a list of significant radiation exposures which have been accumulated this year, through September, for the individuals shown. It is recommended that the appropriate supervision be provided with this information to guide their future actions when work in radiation areas is involved.
>
> "While nobody can give complete assurance that these people will not exceed the permissible level of 12,000mrem for 1959, our exposure history for September indicates that the work areas are well controlled. **Except in the case of Glenn Clayton**, there is enough left in the bank to cover these other employees short of some untoward incident. **"I recommend Glenn Clayton be removed from his present job, and placed in another job, where his radiation exposure would be removed entirely."**

But sadly, the AEC declassified records prove that this did not happen. Glenn not only was kept in his present job, but he worked in all types of jobs with deadly radiation levels for the next eleven years! He was not informed of this previously classified memo written by the radiation safety chief. And he didn't bother to investigate the radiation safety program because in the weekly safety meetings all workers were required to attend, they were assured that elaborate precautions were in place to protect them in this unique field. Glenn believed them.

Years later in April 1968, the Department of Defense and Sandia Laboratory finally published a manual on reentry procedures. By that time, though, Glenn had inhaled and absorbed his lifetime dosage of all types of deadly radiation. Even after those guidelines were issued, during the rehab many workers died early on after they had been overexposed by radiation contamination in the area where they were working.

Radiation safety monitors were there to keep daily radiation exposure records showing the amount of radiation each worker received. That radiation exposure was obtained from the film badge all employees were required to wear.

The standard operating procedure (SOP) said that if a worker went over his allotted exposure, the contractor, Reynolds Electrical and Engineering, Co. (REECo), would send a memo to the Atomic Energy Commission (AEC) requesting radiation exposure limits be *raised*. And the AEC always granted that request.

If workers' radiation exposure went beyond the new radiation exposure limit, the employees with higher radiation exposure levels were often told to "lose your film badge, or we will lay you off." To "lose" one's badge was to *pretend* it was lost, so the supervisors wouldn't have to admit they had knowingly violated established federal safety rules. Maybe *they* decided these workers were expendable!

Three methods were used by the Radiation Safety Department to measure radiation exposure to an employee—the film badge, nasal swabs, and urine samples. The film badge was to detect radiation that penetrated the skin, and nasal swabs and urine samples were to detect radiation that had been inhaled.

Chapter XI

DOCUMENTED NUCLEAR TESTS

A total of 928 *documented* (announced) nuclear tests occurred at the NTS from 1951 to 1992. The first nuclear test conducted at the NTS was code-named Able and detonated onJanuary 27, 1951, and it was a weapons-related airdrop showing a yield of 1kt. The last NTS nuclear weapons test was code-named Divider and detonated on September 23, 1993, with a yield of "less than" 20kt. This was supposedly a test to ensure the safety of US deterrent forces.

Many top secret (undocumented) nuclear tests also occurred at the NTS during that period of time. The nuclear detonations were all given a code name. The government did this so that if they associated the blast with the area itself, it then became classified because it defined the location for certain events.

On August 10, 1957, a zero-yield nuclear safety experiment, number one hundred, code-named Saturn, was detonated in an Area 12 tunnel. Tests were conducted in different tunnel areas that had been driven back into the Area 12 location in Rainier Mesa. The Defense Nuclear Agency (DNA) was attempting to evaluate the effects of nuclear weapons explosions, thermal radiation, blast, shock, X-rays, and gamma rays on military hardware, such as communications equipment, rocket nosecones, and satellites.

To prevent bomb debris and blast from reaching and damaging the experiments, three mechanisms were used to close the blast doors. The first was the fast-acting closure that slammed shut in about one millisecond because of high explosives. The other two closures followed with thirty to three hundred milliseconds. Once radiation safety personnel declared the tunnel safe, workers reentered the tunnel to recover what they could from the experiment. Most of the tunnel nuclear detonations caused major radiation problems.

The first reentry Glenn was involved in was one in B tunnel, code-named Tamalpais, number 168, with a yield of 72kt, and it was detonated on October 8, 1958, as part of the Hardtack II testing program. (The abbreviation kt [kiloton] refers to the energy of nuclear detonation equivalent to the explosive power of a thousand tons of TNT.)

Each series of tests was given a name such as Operation Hardtack II. These Hardtack II tests were comprised of thirty-seven separate detonations, and they were undertaken in a hurry. They were hurried because of a refrain that kept playing in the ears of the AEC, "The moratorium is coming. The moratorium is coming."

Hardtack II tested the various effects possible from combinations of configurations and nuclear yields on military hardware. The government wanted these test completed, and they knew they had precious little time to do so with so ambitious a testing program. The series of nuclear detonations began on September 12, 1958, with the nuclear detonation code-named Otero, number 158, yield 38 tons. And it would conclude on October 30, 1958, with nuclear detonation code-named Titania, number 194, yield 0.2 tons.

As Hardtack concluded, Nuclear Test Ban negotiations were already underway between the United States and the Soviets in Geneva. The moratorium on testing came immediately when the United States finished its Hardtack series in late 1958 and extended until September 1961.

Testing goals for Hardtack II were divided into three categories or objective sets. First was an evaluation on the safety features incorporated into particular nuclear device configurations. Second was to be an examination of how the devices might be stockpiled and how they would react to specific stockpiling procedures. Third—and not entirely separate from the first two—was an assessment of techniques for the *containment* of devices during transport and storage.

This last objective was the one that most involved Glenn and his safety teams. Glenn's job was to take his team into the nuclear bomb detonation area, as soon as rad-safe personnel deemed that reentry back into the tunnel was free enough of contamination to permit human entry.

On his first reentry trip *in*, Glenn was advised by his supervisor that rad-safe personnel had checked radiation levels in the tunnel and indicated no immediate radiation hazard, but the supervisor told him to be alert to the possibility of oxygen depletion. Amazingly, the miners in that early period of testing werenot equipped with breathing apparatus that could have protected them against ingestion of radiation particles or provided an ability to carry sufficient air in an oxygen-deficient environment. One man carried a lit candle not unlike some would in the coal mines of a century earlier to detect a lack of oxygen. It was not a sophisticated device, but it worked. If the candle flame went out, there was no oxygen in the air.

The problem they would confront, however, was that despite elaborate planning and preparation for nuclear explosions, just as at Hiroshima, those who went into the environment after blasts were not provided with what we would have considered adequate personal protection.

Glenn's team was provided no way to detect the presence of explosive or otherwise hazardous gasses. They had gone (cautiously) only a short distance into the tunnel on the teams' very first reentry, and when they lit the candle, it caused a large explosion. Miraculously, no one was seriously injured by the blast, and Glenn counted them lucky that the railroad track on the tunnel floor ran through the large, heavy blast door. Had it not, the door would have been sealed by the blast, trapping him and his crew inside the tunnel without communication with the outside and with diminished oxygen because of the explosion.

Once he had checked his team and established that no one was injured, Glenn had his men get their equipment together, and they reentered the blast area of the tunnel in order to do their work of rehabilitating the area.

Glenn discovered that the blast had dislodged a large boulder from the ceiling in the blast area and that it had fallen onto a ventilation stack with a fan inside it. This equipment had been designed to bring fresh air into the tunnel and exhaust some of the radiation to the outside. This boulder had rendered the exhaust fans inoperative. Glenn got his crew out of there, and no further work could be done until repairs were made to the exhaust fans. Glenn was asked by his manager to personally return again to the contaminated, damaged tunnel to determine if repairs to the exhaust fans could be undertaken with the resources available. Having just survived a potentially fatal explosion in the tunnel, Glenn reentered the blast area with a rad-safe monitor. They had been issued radiation dosimeters that were limited to a two-hour exposure period, and the rad-safe man carried a gamma radiation detector as well. Because of the detector indications, the rad-safe employee refused to go farther into the area at a point about 150 yards from the portal that separated the blast area from the rest of the tunnel.

At this point Glenn had no ability to make determinations of any kind concerning the status of equipment inside the portal. At 150 yards from the blast area, the radiation detector was reading 14 Roentgens (a unit of ionizing radiation) per hour, and both knew they were beyond the *safe* area. The test director wanted data, so Glenn proceeded alone into the highly radiated blast area. When he reached the inoperative fans, he could see that the housing that covered the impellers had been dented sufficiently that the impellers could not rotate. The entire effort took Glenn thirty minutes. He established what damage had been done and estimated the resources necessary for repairs, but his dosimeter had already *pegged* at 2R (radiation consisting of gamma rays) exposure before he could return to the portal and exit the area. The silent, unseen killer had signaled his presence in Glenn as early as that day in 1958.

Why did Glenn risk being in this type of environment? He knew the mining business well, but what he didn't know about was nuclear energy. The radiation numbers, the *lingo*, and the electronic gadgetry were all a mystery to him.

Glenn once recalled that when he exited the tunnel that day, a large number of NTS scientists were waiting for him and his report. They followed his recommendations. The area inside the portal was decontaminated by various means, and the ventilation fans were repaired. B Tunnel had to be completely rehabilitated before the next nuclear bomb could be detonated and tested.

Chapter XII

NUCLEAR BOMB DETONATION PROCEDURES

Before any nuclear bomb was detonated, the testing area was "buttoned up" by security guards who would make sure all employees were out of the area and then duct-tape the trailer doors shut, which gave them the "all clear" sign. Scientists at the control point (CP) would receive the go-ahead from the security department, assuring them that all employees were out of the area. At that time one of the scientists would push the red button, setting off the nuclear detonation. Immediately after a nuclear detonation, some of the employees would have the remainder of the day off. And anytime the workers had some time off, they would head for the casinos in Las Vegas.

After one of the nuclear test Glenn was involved in, when the employees were released, he and his buddy headed to the Sahara Hotel Casino. They were there a very short period of time when they received a phone call to immediately report back to the NTS. Some of the men had been caught in a hydrogen bomb explosion. The men weren't injured, and the AEC chose not to release any information about that initial explosion. The scientists were more concerned about *how soon* the reentry team could get back into the tunnel.

When the workers reentered the tunnel again for rehab, they found the six-by-eight-foot tunnel. The place looked like a bomb blast had occurred!

All of the cable trays mounted on the left side and the wooden trays for all the diagnostic cables were all down, and the vent line was totally destroyed. The workers had no support underground. All utility systems, including air and water, had been destroyed. After Glenn saw the destruction, and the rad-safe monitor checked for radiation contamination, he informed experimenters that he had reassurance that no radiation problem existed; that the blast was strictly a hydrogen gas problem and maybe carbon monoxide, which they could assume. He also assured the experimenters his crew could re-hab that tunnel within two weeks ... or less.

He got volunteers to go back underground with him, and instructed one of his crew members to put portable monitors at various points within the tunnel. Glenn knew the explosive range of hydrogen gas was 6 percent. He had a worker monitoring the machines, and when the range would increase, the workers would evacuate the tunnel.

The next test in the Hardtack II series that Glenn was involved in was the event code-named Evans, detonated on October 29, 1958. It was a fifty-five-ton-yield weapons-related test. Unfortunately for the program, after that nuclear detonation, radiation levels were so high that it was impossible to send men inside the blast portal for data recovery, and that portion of the tunnel was sealed and abandoned.

Just one day later, October 30, 1958, President Eisenhower signed a Testing Moratorium Agreement with the Soviet Union, putting the nuclear testing program on hold. It was supposed to be a banner day for the world, but it was a headache to the US nuclear testing program and the AEC.

Chapter XIII

NIKITA KHRUSHCHEV VISITS USA

With the descent of the Iron Curtain, the Bay of Pigs Invasion, and the conflict in Vietnam lies one of the more bizarre times of the Cold War.

In 1959, not long after signing the Testing Moratorium Agreement, Soviet Premier Nikita Khrushchev planned a goodwill tour to the United States in September. However, the Soviet premier's trip was less than a successful one! To begin with, he specifically wanted to see Disneyland, but for reasons not disclosed, that never happened. From there, the goodwill tour was marked by angry journalists and scantily clad movie stars, and the trip ended in chaos—almost to the point of political farce. Needless to say, the Soviet premier had some very disparaging remarks about the United States.

However, Premier Khrushchev was not so upset that he never wanted to visit the United States again! As a matter of fact, he planned a second trip the next year in 1960! On that visit his own enormous press party accompanied him around the country, and of course, he was met at every stop by almost double the number of correspondents and journalists who were traveling with him.

On this second Khrushchev visit, there was a good deal of discussion on who would handle the logistics for the press party. The White House had a formal organization that was well equipped to handle that kind of thing, but they were aware of all the problems involved, namely the controversy and the difficulties in handling such a huge press party. No one wanted the job!

It was a case of people trying to run away from the hot potato. The big problem was the Soviet premier and Henry Cabot Lodge, his guide on their travels after the Camp David talks were over, spent nearly a week traveling the country. They ended up on the West Coast, where Khrushchev was taken to the filming of *Can-Can*, and he watched a scene where Shirley MacLaine was kicking up her heels. When asked whether he liked that or not, the Soviet premier said, "No, this was obscene. The American's are pornographers."

In May 1960, an international diplomatic crisis erupted when the Union of Soviet Socialist Republic (USSR) shot down an American U-2 spy plane in Soviet airspace and captured its pilot, Francis Gary Powers. The high-altitude U-2 spy plane reconnaissance flights over the USSR gave the United States its first detailed look at the Soviet military facilities.

Confronted with the evidence of his nation's espionage, President Dwight D. Eisenhower was forced to admit to the Soviets that the US Central Intelligence Agency (CIA) had been flying spy missions over the USSR for several years. The Soviets convicted Powers on espionage charges and sentenced him to ten years in prison. The U-2 spy plane incident raised tensions between the United States and the Soviets during the Cold War.

Chapter XIV

MORATORIUM

During the moratorium, testing of nuclear weapons was forbidden, and the majority of employees were laid off because a full workforce was not needed. In reality, they kept thirty out of almost four hundred employees, most of them workers in Area 12, and these men and women went looking for work. However, on a smaller scale, despite the hiatus of nuclear blasts, tunnel reentry continued. The plan was to maintain a small group of professionals who had the capability to rapidly expand to a full workforce should nuclear testing begin again.

REECo kept a small group of highly qualified workers, and because the work at the Nevada Test Site didn't cease, the small workforce began putting in a lot of overtime. The workers in Area 12 were housed in two-man trailers with a bedroom on each end and bathroom in the middle. The men worked long hours in the tunnels and stopped just long enough for meals, showers, and a few hours of sleep. Then they went back to work.

Every other week the workers would make the 110-mile trip from Area 12 to Las Vegas to see their families overnight, and then they hurried back to the base camp very early the next morning. The pace was evidently driven by a sure knowledge that the moratorium would not last very long, and they were going to be ready when that day came. It was an excruciating schedule.

Tunnel reentry meant being exposed to extremely high concentrations of deadly radiation lurking in the blast areas of the tunnels. The Rad-Safe monitor's job was to keep a close watch on radiation exposure on every employee working in the area because they were working in tunnels saturated with deadly radiation. These trusting, patriotic workers were unaware that some of the Rad-Safe monitors were very lax in their job of monitoring radiation and keeping records.

One of the jobs assigned to Glenn during the moratorium was to lead his reentry team back into each tunnel located on Rainier Mesa. All of the tunnels were heavily damaged because of previously conducted nuclear explosions. The scientists wanted all the tunnels totally rehabilitated all the way back to "ground zero" and ready for use when and if the moratorium ended.

On the first tunnel, they drilled a vertical shaft down to the bottom of the cavity that the explosion had formed. They were attempting to determine the outline or shape of the cavity that the nuclear detonation had formed. Glenn was able to determine a rough outline of the glass formed by the blast in the natural silica that was imbedded all through the NTS area. Of course, the glass was highly contaminated with alpha radiation.

During the reentry Glenn and his crew were equipped with respirators and face masks for protection against the deadly radiation and to provide breathable air. But there was a problem. Log books show the temperature in the cavity area was 110 to 120 degrees, and the humidity more than 80 percent. The perspiration caused by the latent conditions caused moisture to render the respirators useless. The very equipment that was intended to protect them became a hazard. Their face masks slipped around on their perspiration-drenched faces, so in order to get their assignment completed, the men sometimes removed clogged respirators and leaking face masks, unwittingly exposing themselves to excessive radiation.

Shortly after that Rainier Mesa tunnel job, Glenn's team was assigned to accomplish a reentry into another tunnel. The Lawrence Livermore Laboratory (LLL) scientists wanted to examine the site where the previous blast had been detonated. As his team excavated their way through the strata leading to the detonation point, they encountered seams and stratus that exceeded 3R readings of radiation. The miners attempted to cover these areas with lead sheeting since they had no means of protection from the radiation.

Next, LLL scientists wanted to create a spherical cavity at the bottom of a vertical shaft so they could bore down into another tunnel. Glenn was called in for the job, which was code-named Linen. The scientists wanted to simulate a nuclear blast by detonating five thousand tons of HE, which equaled five kilotons of conventional explosives. Glenn and his team prepared the tunnel in preparation for the test event. While this work was in progress, the radiation safety monitors discovered that the tunnel was full of radon-thoron radiation. At the time no one knew (including rad-safe monitors) what a safe exposure level to radon might be. So they kept working! But the moratorium ended, and that project was abandoned.

During the moratorium the Soviets were secretly preparing for a major testing campaign. In September 1961, the Soviets broke the treaty with a massive underground nuclear test. A few days later on September 15, 1961, the United States was apparently ready at the same time and resumed nuclear testing at the Nevada Test Site.

Immediately after the moratorium ended, REECo began a big rehiring program. It was almost an overnight buildup in personnel. The workforce mushroomed to about six thousand, and testing resumed. The hurrying to get on with their nuclear testing program required lots of overtime for the rehires. At the NTS, the rehires were ready for the overtime work and the money!

Glenn was then directed to again assist LLL—this time by reentering the tunnel where the last blast, code-named Evans, had been conducted prior to the signing of the moratorium. The LLL scientists wanted to recover a lead encased sample of pure gold that had been a part of the nuclear detonation earlier. The scientists assured Glenn that the canister had been equipped with a one-quarter-inch "tracing" cable that he could simply follow to the pot of gold. The canister, they said, was locked to the cable by a simple one-quarter-inch bolt and nut.

Dying for Answers

Glenn was told he could take the cable off, and he then would be able to easily remove the canister from the drilled hole where it had been placed prior to the blast. He was assured the canister weighed only about twenty-five pounds. After equipping himself for the task as described by the scientists, Glenn and his team entered the tunnel.

Because the radiation levels and tunnel conditions were essentially unknown, Glenn left his crew outside the blast portal and entered the detonation area alone. Based upon what the LLL scientists had told him, one man could easily handle retrieving the canister, even in a contaminated area. The record does not disclose why REECo would not have dispatched a radiation safety monitor with equipment to detect whether or not the team was in danger, but whatever the reason, Glenn went directly into a highly contaminated area without being told that it was saturated with deadly radiation.

When he found the cable, Glenn realized he had not been properly informed about the requirements for the job he faced. He found not a one-quarter-inch cable but rather a three-quarter-inch steel cable. He dug his way along the debris-buried line for about eighty feet into the very center of the underground crater, tracing his way along the cable until he located the end, which was supposed to be attached to the canister with a one-quarter-inch bolt and nut. They turned out to be, like the cable, three-quarter-inch parts too. Luckily, he had brought more than one wrench, so he was able to remove the nut and work the cable away from the canister. That's when he discovered the twenty-five-pound canister of gold encased in lead, which actually weighed more than one hundred pounds.

Glenn knew that the extra time required to complete his task was causing his radiation exposure time to be dramatically increased. He began to carry the canister out of the area. At one point he fell, and the canister landed on his right hand, making a deep gash. He managed to get the canister back to where his team was waiting, and then they carried it out of the tunnel. The scientists started calling the deadly radiation in that area "bowl."

Some days later Glenn learned what "bowl" really was, and it sounded like the scientists were trying to hide the fact that the deadly radiation in that blast area was actually tritium. Glenn learned that he had gotten a very heavy dose of tritium while wrestling with that canister, and so did his crew, even though they were some distance from where Glenn had been.

It is not unreasonable to assume that the canister itself was highly contaminated, and the simple act of carrying it was enough to inject all of them with the deadly enemy they could not see. None of the crew was advised of their overexposure until months later. They wondered why the staff at LLL had been taking three urine samples per week from each worker and having them take what seemed an excessive amount of salt tablets.

Later, the AEC representative provided each member of the team a six-pack of beer they were to drink at the end of their shifts. It was months before they were aware that the *experts* had been trying to flush tritium out of their bodies. One of the workers refused to drink the beer, and when the workers were tested later for radiation contamination, the nondrinker showed a flat line; however, the beer drinkers showed a decline in tritium radiation in the body.

A previously classified Atomic Energy Commission teletype plainly explains the obvious reason these men were overexposed many times to high levels of deadly radiation. The teletype states, "This is necessary in order to meet test schedules and for economic reasons."

What that teletype really says is that ***these workers are expendable!***

This series of nuclear tests ended the Hardtack II series of tests.

Chapter XV

REQUEST TO RAISE EXPOSURE LIMITS

The next series of forty-five nuclear bomb tests were called *Operation Nougat*.

And the next detonation, code-named Antler, number 195, with a 2.6kt yield, was detonated on September 15, 1961. After the nuclear bomb detonation and the reentry team was ready to enter the tunnel, there was a secondary explosion that blew out the portal. No one knew what caused that second blast. The rad-safe monitors reported that the water in the drainage pond next to the highway was reading 72R. The AEC explained this as an "accidental release of radiation detected off site."

The next nuclear shot, code-named Chena, number 198, with a yield stated as being "low," was detonated on October 10, 1961. This test had many radiation problems.

Not much data was recovered because the underground area was extremely contaminated. The only information obtained was a bulletin released by the AEC that announced there was an accidental release of radioactivity detected on site. That meant that the workers were again exposed to deadly radiation.

A teletype from REECo to the AEC, dated November 28, 1961, had a subject line saying, "IMPACT ON TUNNEL ACTIVTIES DUE TO RADIATION CEILINGS." It states,

> "Your instructions that maximum of 3R per quarter must be observed has forced a 75 percent shutdown of tunnel B activities due to insufficient number of underground personnel with little or no radiation exposure for this quarter. All available new hires are being utilized in E tunnel complex. We understand that you can now authorize up to 12R per year for operational necessity, but only 3R per quarter, compared with previous limits of 5R per year and 3R per quarter.

Unless maximum quarterly allowance is increased, the following will result:

Event in tunnel B will be appreciably delayed

1. Future tunnel events will likely be delayed. Nature of delay indeterminate at this time and dependent on problem which might be encountered. Accident potential greatly increased due to inability to work new green hires along with experienced miners in tunnels having radiation levels.
2. We may be forced to retain large numbers of underground personnel on the payroll in a non-productive capacity awaiting expiration of maximum allowable dosage period or opening of new underground facilities. The latter required, in most instances, a four to six week period from time of new tunnel authorization to time of full utilization of miners.

We urgently request that approximately 30 key personnel now working in B tunnel, all of whom have exceeded or are about to exceed 3R for the quarter, be allowed to continue working in B tunnel. This is considered necessary if we are to meet test schedules and is highly desirable from an economic standpoint, as well as the morale of this group of men, and safety of other workmen.

We further request that the quarterly maximum allowable dosage be increased to at least 5R with the total of 12R per year. These dosages could be at the discretion of the Test Manager to fulfill operational needs and spot requirements. List of 30 men now working in B tunnel with exposures for the quarter and year shown below. We estimate maximum exposure to the people to be 300MR per week for the next 3 to 4 weeks. Glenn's name was listed at the bottom of that teletype.

A nuclear detonation two months later, code-named Feather, number 204, with a 150kt yield, was detonated three days before Christmas on December 22, 1961.

This blast caused many severe radiation problems. In fact, officials decided to try to maintain ventilation by turning on fans inside the tunnel to get rid of the radiation into the atmosphere rather than keeping it in the work area. A ventilation duct was laid on the mesa above the tunnel, and workers drilled a hole from the tunnel to the mesa. After the nuclear event was executed, it was Glenn's job to go with one rad-safe employee to the mesa to determine if the ventilation system was functional. When the two men got to the mesa, Glenn found that the ground motion from the blast had broken the ventilation pipe at many seams, rendering it useless. The rad-safe employee told Glenn that it was safe for him to do his work there because his radiation monitor was only reading a few R and the wind was blowing away from them.

The rad-safe employee left, and while he was gone, the wind changed direction. Now it was coming right over the ventilation pipe toward Glenn, which he was unaware of. When the rad-safe employee returned, he reported the radiation levels on the net to the control station personnel below.

Glenn was ordered to leave the mesa immediately as soon as control personnel heard the radiation levels, which were extremely high at that time. He had already exceeded his yearly radiation dosage, and was working on a waiver. The AEC issued waivers for any employee who had already reached their maximum allowed radiation exposure. *Unknown to Glenn, it is obvious the AEC considered him expendable!* In regards to the nuclear detonation two months earlier, code-named Chena, Glenn was not allowed to work inside the tunnel area, but rad-safe directed him to supervise and direct his crew from outside the tunnel. His radiation exposure at that point was off the charts. Somehow, he magically qualified to work inside the tunnel two months later on the "Feather" nuclear detonation. Nuclear test code-named Danny Boy, number 216, with 430 tons of explosives, was detonated on March 5, 1962. It made a crater with a diameter of 265 feet and a depth of eighty-four feet. *Crater* is defined as "a nuclear device placed shallow enough underground to produce a throw-out of earth when exploded." AEC only released the following information: "Accidental release of radioactivity detected off site only." This most likely translates to "more deadly radiation exposure to workers."

RG — U.S. ATOMIC ENERGY
COMMISSION
Location **LANL**
Collection Records Center
Folder

INCOMING

TWX NR C-43 282125Z

FM REYNOLDS ELEC & ENGR CO LAS VEGAS NEV
TO JAMES E REEVES/USAEC OFO ALBUQUERQUE NMEX
INFO MILTON REX/USAEC OFO LAS VEGAS NEV
JAMES OLSEN/LRL MERCURY NEV
DR WM OGLE/LASL LOS ALAMOS NMEX
BRIG GEN A W BETTS/USAEC DMA WASHDC
AEC GRNC
BT

Dist:
Orig-Ogle
CC-Shipman
CC-Graves
CC-Freeman/Hoyt
CC-J.Hall
NEB
CCNewman
CC-File

SUBJECT - IMPACT ON TUNNEL ACTIVITIES DUE TO RADIATION CEILINGS
REF LETTERS CMM J R CROCKETT TO JAMES E REEVES CMM DATED NOV 17, 1961
AND C S MAUPIN TO JAMES E REEVES CMM DATED NOVEMBER 15, 1961
YOUR INSTRUCTIONS THAT MAXIMUM OF 3R PER QUARTER MUST BE OBSERVED
HAS FORCED A 75 PERCENT SHUTDOWN OF TUNNEL B ACTIVITIES DUE TO
INSUFFICIENT NUMBER OF UNDERGROUND PERSONNEL WITH LITTLE OR NO RADIATION
EXPOSURE FOR THIS QUARTER PD ALL AVAILABLE NEW HIRES ARE BEING UTILIZED
IN "E" TUNNEL COMPLEX PD WE UNDERSTAND THAT YOU CAN NOW AUTHORIZE UP TO
12R PER YEAR FOR OPERATIONAL NECESSITY BUT ONLY 3R PER QUARTER COMPARED
WITH PREVIOUS LIMITS OF 5R PER YEAR AND 3R PER QUARTER PD

RECEIVED
NOV 28 1961
Los Alamos
Scientific Laboratory
P.O. Box 1663
Mail & Records

COPIED/DOE
LANL RC

CLASSIFICATION CANCELLED
BY AUTHORITY OF DOE/OC

PAGE TWO NR C-43

UNLESS MAXIMUM QUARTERLY ALLOWANCE IS INCREASED CMM THE FOLLOWING WILL RESULT CLN

1. EVENT IN B.08 WILL BE APPRECIABLY DELAYED PD
2. FUTURE TUNNEL EVENTS WILL LIKELY BE DELAYED PD NATURE OF DELAY INDETERMINATE AT THIS TIME AND DEPENDENT ON PROBLEM WHICH MIGHT BE ENCOUNTERED PD
3. ACCIDENT POTENTIAL GREATLY INCREASED DUE TO INABILITY TO WORK NEW OR GREEN HIRES ALONG WITH EXPERIENCED MINERS IN TUNNELS HAVING RADIATION LEVELS PD
4. WE MAY BE FORCED TO RETAIN LARGE NUMBERS OF UNDERGROUND PERSONNEL ON THE PAYROLL IN A NON-PRODUCTIVE CAPACITY AWAITING EXPIRATION OF MAXIMUM ALLOWABLE DOSAGE PERIOD OR OPENING OF NEW UNDERGROUND FACILITIES PD THE LATTER REQUIRES CMM IN MOST INSTANCES CMM A FOUR TO SIX WEEK PERIOD FROM TIME OF NEW TUNNEL AUTHORIZATION TO TIME OF FULL UTILIZATION OF MINERS PD

WE URGENTLY REQUEST THAT APPROXIMATELY 30 KEY PERSONNEL NOW WORKING IN "B" TUNNEL CMM ALL OF WHOM HAVE EXCEEDED OR ARE ABOUT TO EXCEED 3R FOR THE QUARTER CMM BE ALLOWED TO CONTINUE WORKING IN "B" TUNNEL PD THIS IS CONSIDERED NECESSARY IF WE ARE TO MEET TEST SCHEDULES AND IS HIGHLY DESIRABLE FROM AN ECONOMIC STANDPOINT AS WELL AS THE MORALE OF THIS GROUP OF MEN AND SAFETY OF OTHER WORKMEN PD

PAGE THREE NR C-43

WE FURTHER REQUEST THAT THE QUARTERLY MAXIMUM ALLOWABLE DOSAGE BE INCREASED TO AT LEAST 5R WITH THE TOTAL OF 12R PER YEAR PD THESE DOSAGES COULD BE AT THE DESCRETION OF THE TEST MANAGER TO FULFILL OPERATIONAL NEEDS AND SPOT REQUIREMENTS PD LIST OF 30 MEN NOW WORKING IN "B" TUNNEL WITH EXPOSURES FOR THE QUARTER AND YEAR SHOWN BELOW PD WE ESTIMATE MAXIMUM EXPOSURE TO THE PEOPLE TO BE 300 MR PER WEEK FOR THE NEXT 3 TO 4 WEEKS PD

NAME	QUARTERLY	YEARLY
GLEN CLAYTON	3,930	4,675

Chapter XVI

CONTAMIMATED ABOVE TOLERANCE

On April 14, 1962, a nuclear detonation with the code name Platte, number 225, with a 1.85kt yield, was detonated. It was a weapons-related, tunnel shaft test. That nuclear blast was a bad one. It split that line of sight pipe all the way from the mesa, and it split the mountain open. Fallout venting through a series of holes that the explosion had opened from the tunnel to the face of the mesa. Venting from the portal was also evident. Radiation lurking in that tunnel was very deadly. So deadly, in fact, that the Rad-Safe logbook notes on the reentry, that on the swing shift, "Film badges changed, and survey made of all personnel. Twelve people were contaminated above tolerance. One worker had a high radiation reading in his hair. These people were escorted to the Area 12 change house for the decontamination operation, and they were released after two or three trips through the shower. That was very important to wash the contamination off the skin, however, nothing could be done about the contamination inhaled by the workers. The AEC explains there was "accidental release of radioactivity detected off site." There was no mention of the "onsite radioactivity" or the workers who were escorted to the Area 12 change house to be decontaminated.

Another nuclear detonation that was code-named Des Moines, number 253, with a 2.9kt yield, was detonated on June 13, 1962. Shortly after the bomb was detonated, an evacuation order was issued, warning everyone to leave the area immediately! The only way to exit the area was a two-lane gravel road. However, people evacuating that area made it a four-lane, one-way road in order to *get out of Dodge fast!* One of the scientists was standing in a close filming area, capturing the aftermath of the event, when everything began blowing out of the tunnel. The scientist overheard a couple of miners rushing to their vehicles and saying, "We worked all night putting more than three thousand sandbags in that tunnel ... and there they all go!" AEC announced to the public, "Accidental release of radioactivity detected off site." Maybe they should have warned the employees to watch out for flying sandbags!

Chapter XVII

NUCLEAR TESTING DURING CUBAN MISSILE CRISIS

The next fifty-two tests were all categorized under *Operation Storax*. A DOD nuclear test code-named Marshmallow, number 261, with a "low" yield, was detonated on June 2, 1962. There's no information on this except the DOE's response, "Accidental release of radioactivity detected onsite only." More workers were contaminated by cancer causing radiation exposure. A crater detonation code name Sedan, number 264, was detonated on July 6, 1962, with a 104kt yield. It was an excavation experiment and caused a crater 1,280 feet in diameter and 320 feet deep. It was a thermonuclear device, and radioactivity was detected off-site. Three short months after the Sedan detonation, the United States and the Soviet Union engaged in a tense thirteen-day political and military standoff called the Cuban Missile Crisis in October 1962. After seizing power in the Caribbean island nation of Cuba in 1959, leftist revolutionary leader Fidel Castro aligned himself with the Soviet Union. Under Castro, Cuba grew dependent on the Soviets for military and economic aid.

The Cuban Missile Crisis began over the installation of nuclear-armed Soviet missiles on Cuba, which was just ninety miles from US shores. The two superpowers plunged into one of their biggest Cold War confrontations after the pilot of the American U-2 spy plane made a high-altitude pass over Cuba on October 14, 1962, and photographed a Soviet

SS-4 medium-range ballistic missile being assembled for installation. President Kennedy was briefed about the situation on October 16, and he immediately called together a group of advisors and officials known as the Executive Committee (or ExCom). For the next two weeks, President Kennedy and his team wrestled with a diplomatic crisis of epic proportions.

In a TV address on October 22, 1962, President John Kennedy notified Americans about the presence of the missiles, explained his decision to enact a naval blockade around Cuba, and made it clear that the United States was prepared to use military force—if necessary—to neutralize this threat to our national security. Many people feared the world was on the brink of a nuclear war. However, the disaster was avoided when the United States agreed to Soviet leader Nikita Khrushchev's offer to remove the Cuban missiles in exchange for the promise that the United States would not invade Cuba. For the American officials, the urgency of the situation stemmed from the fact that the nuclear-armed Cuban missiles were being installed so close to the US mainland. From that launch point, they were capable of quickly reaching targets in the eastern United States.

If they had become operational, the missiles would greatly altered the scope of the nuclear rivalry between the United States and the Soviet Union. Soviet leader Nikita Khrushchev had gambled on sending the missiles to Cuba with the specific goal of increasing his nation's nuclear strike capability. From the outset of the crisis, Kennedy and ExCom determined that the presence of Soviet missiles in Cuba was unacceptable. The challenge facing them was to orchestrate their removal without initiating a wider conflict and inciting the possibility of a nuclear war. President Kennedy ultimately decided to employ the US Navy to establish a blockade of the island of Cuba to prevent the Soviets from delivering additional missiles and military equipment. Second, he would deliver an ultimatum that the existing missiles be removed.

A crucial moment in the unfolding crisis came on October 24, 1962, when Soviet ships bound for Cuba neared the line of US vessels enforcing the blockade. Had the Soviets attempted to breach the blockade, it would have likely sparked a military confrontation that would have quickly escalated to a nuclear exchange. But the Soviet ships stopped short of the blockade. Despite enormous tension, Soviet and American leaders found a way out of the impasse. On October 26, 1962, Khrushchev sent a message to Kennedy, and he offered to remove the Cuban missiles if US leaders promised not to invade Cuba.

The Kennedy administration decided to accept Khrushchev's offer. Attorney General Robert Kennedy personally delivered the message to the Soviet ambassador in Washington, and on October 28, 1962, the crisis drew to a close. Both the United States and the Soviet Union were sobered by the Cuban Missile Crisis. The following year, a direct hotline communication link was installed between Washington and Moscow to help defuse similar situations. The two superpowers signed treaties related to nuclear weapons. The Cold War was far from over. The crisis also convinced the Soviets to increase their investment in an arsenal of intercontinental ballistic missiles capable of reaching the United States from Soviet territory. Nuclear testing never stopped at the Nevada Test Site during the Cuban Missile Crisis. In 1962, several nuclear detonations revealed radioactivity detected on-site as well as off-site, however, the DOE would release no other information.

Chapter XVIII

THE YUBA EVENT

The next nuclear detonation, code-named Yuba, number 326, had a yield of 3.1kt, and it was detonated on June 5, 1963. A crew of rehabilitation workers was sent back into the tunnel after they were told there was no radiation present. They worked an eight-hour shift, and as they exited the tunnel afterward, they walked through a gate with radiation detectors attached on both sides of the walkway. Both alarms sounded loudly. After a radiation safety check showed high levels of contamination to the tunnel workers, they were taken to Donner Laboratory in Los Angeles, California, where they were placed in a room with lead walls for one week as they detoxed. They had all been overexposed to excessive amounts of deadly iodine.

In the declassified records released by the DOE through the Freedom of Information Act, there was a memo dated July 3, 1963, from the AEC to REECo, and it states, "We request the name, social security number, job title, place of birth and date of birth, on all persons involved in the Yuba event." Employees learned, at that time, that the AEC had been keeping mortality charts on all of the Nevada Test Site tunnel workers. Glenn's name was on that list, even though earlier a DOE employee had denied that Glenn was involved in the Yuba event. A few months before his death, Glenn wrote a ten-page work history detailing many events and radiation problems in his almost thirty years of employment with REECo. There, he documented his involvement in the Yuba event.

Another glaring clue about the DOE cover-up of Glenn's true radiation exposure includes the missing film badge records, especially those from June 7, 1963, to July 29, 1963. And what occurred in that time period? The Yuba nuclear blast, which they began calling "the Yuba Incident." It's just a matter of fact that when film badges were *lost*, the radiation readings for that employee greatly diminished. The recorded radiation exposure for an individual on his DOE radiation exposure history would show much less radiation exposure for the employee. Obviously, if someone was involved in an *incident* during a period when no film badge record is available, it would be more advantageous for the company to assume no exposure despite the fact that the person was present in an environment of hazardous radiation exposure.

Chapter XIX

PRESIDENT KENNEDY ASSASSINATION

The next forty-two nuclear detonation were under *Operation Niblick*.

An underground tunnel blast with a yield of 249kt, code-named Bilby, number 336, was detonated on September 13, 1963. It was the first nuclear tunnel detonation reported to have been felt in Las Vegas. The AEC released no other information. Some progress was made in easing Cold War tensions when John F. Kennedy was president of the United States and Nikita Khrushchev was premier of Soviet Russia. In 1963, the two sides reached a major arms control agreement. They agreed to ban the testing of nuclear weapons above ground, underwater, and in space. So too, they established a direct telephone line between the White House and the Kremlin.

On November 22, 1963, a nuclear device code-named Greys, number 346, with a yield listed as "intermediate," was detonated in an Area 12 shaft location. No information was released regarding its radioactivity.

A few hours later on that same day, the entire United States was in shock and disbelief when word blasted over radios that President John F. Kennedy had been assassinated. At first, workers at the NTS thought it was a hoax. Then when the report was verified, everyone felt the shock. Tears came to the eyes of many workers. Some prayed, and everyone asked, "Why"?

It was 11:35 a.m. at the NTS. All work ceased, and employees were sent home.

Shortly before this tragedy, by the fall of 1963, President John F. Kennedy and his political advisers were preparing for the next presidential campaign. Although he had not formally announced his candidacy, it was clear that President Kennedy was going to run again, and he seemed confident about his chances for reelection.

Then on November 12, he held the first important political planning session for the upcoming election year. At the meeting JFK stressed the importance of winning Florida and Texas and talked about his plans to visit both states in the next two weeks. Mrs. Kennedy would accompany him on the swing through Texas, which would mark her first extended public appearance since the loss of their baby, Patrick, in August. On November 21, the president and first lady departed on Air Force One for the two-day, five-city tour of Texas.

President Kennedy seemed to relish the prospect of leaving Washington, getting out among the people and into the political fray. The first stop was San Antonio. Vice-President Lyndon B. Johnson, Governor John B. Connelly, and Senator Ralph W. Yarborough led the welcoming party. They accompanied the president to Brooks Air Force Base for the dedication of the Aerospace Medical Health Center. Continuing on to Houston, he addressed a Latin American citizens' organization and spoke at a testimonial dinner for Congressman Albert Thomas before ending the day in Fort Worth.

A light rain was falling on Friday morning, November 22, but a crowd of several thousand stood in the parking lot outside the Texas hotel where the Kennedys had spent the night. A platform was set up, and the president, who was wearing no protection against the weather, came out to make some brief remarks. "There are no faint hearts in Fort Worth," he began, "and I appreciate your being here this morning. Mrs. Kennedy is organizing herself. It takes longer, but of course, she looks better than we do when she does it." He went on to talk about the nation's need for being "second to none" in defense and in space, for continued growth in the economy, and for "the willingness of the citizens of the United States to assume the burdens of leadership."

The presidential party left the hotel and went by motorcade to Carswell Air Force Base for the thirteen-minute flight to Dallas. Arriving at Love Field, the president and Mrs. Kennedy disembarked and immediately walked toward a fence where a crowd of well-wishers had gathered, and they spent several minutes shaking hands.

The first lady received a bouquet of red roses, which she brought with her to the waiting limousine. Governor John Connolly and his wife, Nellie, were already seated in the open convertible as the Kennedys entered and sat behind them. Since it was no longer raining, the plastic bubble top had been left off. The vice president and Mrs. Johnson occupied another car in the motorcade.

The procession left the airport and traveled along a ten-mile route that wound through downtown Dallas on the way to the Trade Mart, where the president was scheduled to speak at a luncheon. Crowds of excited people lined the streets and waved to the Kennedys. The car turned off Main Street at Dealey Plaza around 12:30 p.m. As it was passing the Texas School Book Depository, gunfire suddenly reverberated in the plaza. Bullets struck the president's neck and head, and he slumped over toward Mrs. Kennedy. The governor was also hit in the chest.

The car sped off to Parkland Memorial Hospital just a few minutes away. But little could be done for the president. A Catholic priest was summoned to administer the last rites, and at 1:00 p.m., President John F. Kennedy was pronounced dead. Though seriously wounded, Governor Connolly would recover.

The president's body was brought to Love Field and placed on Air Force One. Before the plane took off, a grim-faced Lyndon B. Johnson stood in the tight, crowded compartment and took the oath of office, administered by US District Court Judge Sarah Hughes. The brief ceremony took place at 2:38 p.m.

Less than an hour earlier, police had arrested Lee Harvey Oswald, a recently hired employee at the Texas School Book Depository. He was being held for the assassination of President Kennedy and the fatal shooting of Patrolman J. D. Tippit on a Dallas street shortly afterward.

On Sunday morning, November 24, Oswald was scheduled to be transferred from police headquarters to the county jail. Viewers across America watching the live television coverage suddenly saw a man aim a pistol and fire at point-blank range. The assailant was identified as Jack Ruby, a local nightclub owner. Oswald died two hours later at Parkland Hospital.

Chapter XX

On Monday morning, November 25, 1963, nuclear bomb testing resumed at the Nevada Test Site.

Nuclear detonations code-named Barracuda and Sardine, number 347, were detonated on December 4, 1963, with an indicated "low" yield range. At that time the scientists were experimenting with conducting two nuclear detonations simultaneously located in two tunnel shafts, one on top of the other. All of those detonations reported, "Accidental release of radioactivity detected onsite." No other information released.

Nuclear detonations continued under *Operation Whetstone* and *Operation Flintlock*.

A total of ninety-four nuclear detonations occurred at the Nevada Test Site in 1964 and 1965. Of these detonations, twenty-two of the nuclear blasts recorded radiation leakage. A total of fourteen of those blasts detected radiation on-site. And total of eight detected radiation off-site. Nuclear detonation code-named Rex, number 442, was detonated on February 24, 1966. It was a weapons-related low-yield test with a yield of less than 20kt. No information was released by the AEC.

On March 5, 1966, nuclear detonation number 443, code-named Red Hot, with a yield of less than 20kt, was detonated. Glenn commented on the reentry of that blast.

> That was one of the strangest re-entries I ever made. We walked back in that tunnel, and the total tunnel was just orange glass. The railroad track was vaporized, and the ground support sets, where they were, was a grey mark across the tunnel about every eight feet, which was all that was left of the ground support sets. We got back to what was a 30 foot long bunker built out of four foot thick, reinforced concrete. We got back there, and it was just a pile of rubble. They had placed a wedge-shaped gas seal before the shot. That shot just took it right on through. It didn't hold at all. Drove it right through. And the glass … you couldn't believe it. We managed to get back to the cavity edge and everything was just orange and yellow glass. The man who designed the wedge-shaped seal said that "this will seal it up good" … but it took the whole wall out! In fact, you couldn't even tell where the wedge had been. The blast just smoothed the tunnel walls totally. We never did find that wedge.
>
> A lot of the samples were buried under the floor of the tunnel, in drill holes, and the explosion didn't damage those things very much. They were recovered. Some of the cameras were recovered, and even damaged, they got the film out of them. I guess from the beginning, up through a period of time, there was a hell of a learning curve.
>
> I think that was another reason for making a lot of the re-entries. They were trying to analyze what the failure modes were, and see if they could take measures to prevent the failures. It wasn't very many years before they were successful.

Another nuclear detonation, code-named Piledriver, number 462, with a 62kt yield, was detonated on June 2, 1966. This one completely tore up the access shaft to the collar. It upheaved the ground at the surface twelve feet back around the ground zero, which was 1,500 feet from the shaft collar. It did a lot of surface spall. (*Spall* means it actually split the ground and did a lot of damage.) Glenn and his crew were able to mine back down into Piledriver and reenter the test drifts to ascertain the survival of the different configurations of hardening that had occurred. The DOD announced, "Accidental release of radio-activity detected onsite only." That equates to saying, "Workers contaminated once again."

From 1963 to 1969, Glenn was also involved in reentries in the nuclear detonations code-named Marshmallow, Gumdrop, Door Mist, Tiny Tot, and Midi Mist. All of these events had radiation leakage at some point. One of the main problems with radiation leakage was seen through the cables. At the outset there was leakage of high radiation levels coming through the cables themselves. All workers involved in reentry and rehabilitating the tunnels were exposed to the deadly radiation present in those areas.

Chapter XXI

ALL EYES ON FLORIDA

While a lot of the country had their eyes on Florida, where we were trying to win another race with Russia and land first on the moon, crews of men were entering extremely dangerous unknowns, doing it with just a small amount of scientific knowledge to back them. Were they just doing it for the money? Absolutely not! Most of these workers were WWII veterans, and they were doing this for the national defense of the United States.

Their country needed the information from these nuclear tests so that we could build defense systems that would withstand nuclear blasts. And don't be fooled—the Russians were trying to take over the world then. So these people entered hot radioactive tunnels just so we could remain free and aim our sights at the moon.

On October 10, 1968, nuclear blast number 567, code-named Vat, was detonated. The only information given said that it was a weapons-related shaft detonation of less than 20kt.

The very next day at Cape Canaveral, Florida, the United States sent the first crewed flight into space with Apollo 7. It achieved its goal of a manned lunar landing despite the major setback of a 1967 Apollo 1 cabin fire that killed the entire crew during a prelaunch test.

After the first landing, sufficient flight hardware remained for nine follow-up landings with a plan for extended lunar geological and astrophysical exploration. Budget cuts forced the cancelation of three of these flights. Five of the remaining six missions achieved success.

Meanwhile, back at the NTS, the nuclear bomb testing continued on a daily basis. Many days more than one nuclear device was detonated. With each test, more was learned, and more men were contaminated with deadly, cancer-causing radiation.

On May 26, 1970, nuclear detonation number 651, code-named Hudson Moon, with a yield of less than 20kt, was detonated. The day after that nuclear blast, the reentry crew went back into the blast area. As soon as they entered the area, they were directed by rad-safe to take off their personal clothes and put on two pair of coveralls furnished by the AEC. This was an effort to partially shield the team from the deadly radiation lingering in the tunnel. After the tunnel job was completed, workers put their personal clothing back on and exited the tunnel.

Nuclear tests at the Nevada Test Site were 'documented'(information released to the public) or 'undocumented'(information not released to the public). One of the documented nuclear tests that was announced, suddenly, after the blast, became "top secret." The test, code-named Baneberry, number 666, with a 10kt yield, was detonated on December 18, 1970. The nuclear bomb was detonated at 270 meters below the surface. It blew a large hole in the top of the mountain, and heavy amounts of radiation escaped into the atmosphere. The scientists were always very sensitive about the wind direction before they detonated a bomb. They didn't want the winds blowing to the south toward Las Vegas. On this occasion, after the bomb was detonated, the winds suddenly changed direction, and the radiation cloud started moving toward Las Vegas.

The NTS engineers and scientists panicked. The team in Las Vegas was warned they may have to evacuate the building. But in a short while, the winds shifted again and headed back toward the NTS and the Utah state line. Heavy radiation levels reached Utah sheep herds feeding in that area. As a result, all the sheep were covered in deadly radiation and died shortly after they were exposed. The government quickly—and very generously—paid the sheep owners for their losses.

The men working in that blast area were told to remove all of their clothing and put on clothing issued to them by the AEC. Their clothing along with their vehicles were buried. The fallout also rained down in the local area, affecting eighty-six workers at the NTS. Although the DOE stated that none of them had been harmed, two of the workers died four years later from leukemia. A worker who was driving one of the trucks in that area shortly after the blast was diagnosed with bone and lung cancer. He died a horrible, painful death seven months later. The deadly radioactive cloud could be seen in Las Vegas. The dust reached a height of around three kilometers, and from there it was carried by winds into several adjacent US states. After the Baneberry incident, nuclear testing at the NTS was suspended for six months pending investigation. The official report issued by the AEC Commission concluded that the primary cause of the venting was "an unexpected and unrecognized abnormally high water content in the medium surrounding the detonation point."

The next tunnel nuclear detonation, code-named Camphor, number 671, was detonated on June 29, 1971. On the "Evaluation of Clayton" records, someone made a note that siad, "Film badge card #009208, shows radiation exposure to Gamma 50, Beta 95, and also lists Glenn's date of birth. This was a *handwritten* film badge card." It was the one and only *handwritten* film badge card in his many years of employment. All other film badge cards were machine-printed. AEC released this information on the test, "Accidental release of radioactivity detected on site only."

Chapter XXII

MULTIPLE NUCLEAR DETONATIONS

On September 22, 1971, the DOE decided to experiment with detonating four nuclear bombs in separate holes simultaneously. These four holes were code-named Frijoles-Deming, Frijoles-Espuela, Frijoles-Guaje, and Frijoles-Petaca. It was number 680, and documents show the yield was less than 20kt each. Scientists considered these blasts successes; however, the DOE released no information at all.

At the NTS, the type of deadly radiation is called "ionizing radiation." Ionizing radiation exposure can cause acute effects or delayed effects. Delayed radiation effects occur years or decades after long-term radiation exposure. Cancer and genetic effects are examples of delayed effects. Studies of people exposed to ionizing radiation show that there's an increased risk for developing many types of cancer, including cancers of the blood, brain, lymph system, stomach, lung, liver, colon, bladder, breast, ovaries, thyroid, and skin.

There were other hazards in addition to the radiation in the NTS tunnels. Mining in and of itself is a relatively hazardous occupation, but with the added requirements at NTS, it was deadly. Cave-ins from the stressed strata inside the tunnels after the nuclear detonations were not unusual occurrences. Just the vibrations from walking could instigate little and occasionally large earth movements.

Glenn told of one occasion when he was walking with one of his crew. He noticed a large boulder had come loose from high up on the tunnel wall, and rubble was beginning to fall on the worker walking with him. Glenn reached for the boulder and was able to hold it up just long enough for the worker to get hold of it. Together, they managed to set it on the ground, and neither one of them got hurt. It was documented that one worker died when a large boulder fell on him and crushed him.

Today we are all familiar with the hazards associated with the handling of materials containing asbestos. In the 1960s, Glenn and his crew routinely wrapped cables in the detonation areas far underground with asbestos batting, and then after a detonation, their job included removing the often shredded asbestos wraps. They were not equipped with safety equipment of any kind because no one knew the danger of asbestos in those days.

One thing the AEC seemed very protective of was their image. They always made sure the accidents involving workers on the job, especially when they led to the death of a worker, were not made public. Once, a large hole had been drilled 1,500 feet down for the placement of a nuclear bomb. After the day shift finished work, the hole was to be covered with a large steel plate for protection. Two of the workers were attempting to place the steel plate over the hole when one of the workers accidently backed into the opening. Management assumed the worker could not possibly survive a fall like that, so they immediately filled in the hole and closed that area permanently.

Another death involved a worker standing in one of the newly drilled tunnels. For an unknown reason, the ground under him collapsed, and he fell several feet and was badly injured. He was transported to a hospital in Las Vegas, and he died a short time later. Doctors said, "He would have died within a few weeks anyway because he was full of cancer."

Chapter XXIII

TRANSFERRED TO LOS ALAMOS, AREA 3

In 1971, Glenn was promoted to department manager and was transferred to Area 3, where he took over the Los Alamos Scientific Laboratory (LASL) construction effort for the down-hole nuclear bomb testing. This involved testing a nuclear bomb placed at the bottom of a hole several hundred feet deep in the desert floor. This type of nuclear bomb detonation was new. Large cranes were used to lower the nuclear bomb into the newly drilled hole, exactly to Los Alamos Scientific Laboratory (LASL) specifications. After the bomb was detonated, the crane operator would place his crane over the hole, where radiation was escaping into the atmosphere, and bring the device to the surface. Then the crew would hand over the device to the LASL scientists for further testing.

The crane operator was continually exposed to heavy amounts of radiation coming from that hole. One of the crane operators developed bone and lung cancer, and after receiving a few months of chemotherapy, he died a very painful death in less than a year. Many attempted to stop the pain associated with bone cancer, but small doses of morphine didn't work very well. That worker would lie on the floor, writhing in pain for hours at a time. He was finally hospitalized, and heavy doses of morphine became his constant friend, putting him in a semiconscious state of bliss. At least then the pain was bearable. He asked for a preacher to come and talk with him. His words to this preacher were overwhelming. He asked, "I know how to live, pastor, but I need you to tell me how to die."

Dot Clayton

LASL was experimenting with deeper and deeper configurations of downhole drilling. Glenn was sent to Manitowoc, Wisconsin, to purchase the largest crane ever built with rubber tires. All other cranes in use in Area 3 at the time were not as big and were on steel tracks. The Manitowoc crane was the largest the NTS operators had ever seen. When it arrived at the NTS, the operators named it "Big Blue." A train hauled that big blue monster on twelve flatbed railroad cars from Manitowoc, Wisconsin, to Las Vegas, Nevada, where flatbed trucks were then used to transport the crane in sections to Area 3.

Arguments began immediately among the crane operators over which one would be the first to operate Big Blue.

Regrettably, the first operator became one of the statistics when he later developed lung and bone cancer and suffered a painful death. No radiation exposure records were made public at that time, so this first crane operator never knew what caused his cancers. And he certainly would never have guessed that it was from the deadly radiation he was breathing into his body and absorbing through his skin.

Chapter XXIV

SURVEILLANCE AFTER DETONATION

Another fatality of the Cold War nuclear bomb testing at the NTS involved a helicopter pilot. Here is an excerpt from a letter he wrote shortly before his death:

> "Radiation is imperceptible to human senses: an area that is deadly looks, sounds, smells and feels exactly like it is perfectly safe. Injury from radiation is cumulative—the longer the exposure, the more damage. Thus it is always vital to know whether you're being irradiated.
>
> Most of the people who worked around nuclear devices for the United States Government, or their contractors were kept in the dark when their supervisors knew for sure, or had a pretty good idea they were sending the workers into work areas that were potentially deadly.
>
> I was on duty at the Nevada Test Site working for EG&G Energy Measurements, who was contracted by the Department of Energy, on March 22, 1986. I was ordered to do low recon after the Glenco nuclear detonation. I flew as low as 50 feet over ground zero, and my mission was to see if there was any visual evidence that a shot had vented.

Many years later I learned that it had vented. I was either too patriotic or too stupid to know I was in great danger of radiation.

I was on duty again at the Nevada Test Site working for EG&G on April 10, 1986. I was ordered to recon the Mighty Oak nuclear detonation. The DOD recorded, "Controlled release of radioactivity detected offsite". Even though I have suffered emotionally and physically, I stand humble before some of my fellow workers and their families who have suffered greater losses, having lost their loved ones. In most cases we workers did not even know we were being exposed to such deadly nuclear poison, but many of our supervisors did, AND the Atomic Energy Commission did."

The Glenco nuclear detonation, number 975, with a 29kt yield, was detonated on March 22, 1986. Notes from the DOE on that nuclear blast state, "Operational release of radioactivity detected off site." And this release was most likely directed into the cockpit of that helicopter hovering right above the blast area.

The Mighty Oak nuclear detonation, number 976, was detonated on April 10, 1986. It was a DOD test with a yield of "less than 20kt." The DOD commented, "Controlled release of radioactivity detected off site." Again, I'm sure this release went right into the cockpit of that helicopter hovering above the blast area.

This patriotic former soldier and helicopter pilot was given no protective apparatus to wear. The doors on his helicopter had been removed to give him better vision, he was told, of the areas his helicopter was required to hover over after a nuclear blast. But without the doors, it was impossible to close the cockpit for his safety and lessen his exposure to the deadly radiation that was escaping into the atmosphere ... and the cockpit of his helicopter. He first got cancer of the eye, and his right eye had to be removed. That, of course, caused him to lose his pilot's license ... and his job. Shortly after his eye was removed, he developed lung cancer and died.

All of these dedicated and patriotic workers faced an enemy they could not see and could not destroy, one that would not go away. We've all heard war stories about our soldiers being sent into hazardous areas to complete jobs, their superiors knowing full well that there was more than a good chance they would not return. They were considered *expendable*! But with these NTS workers, most of whom had served in WWII, they didn't consider the job at the NTS to be hazardous. They considered this a necessary job, and once again, these men and women would help our country. But they had no idea they would be risking their lives. Those brave workers died without knowing the extent of the cover-up perpetrated by our government regarding their almost daily exposure to deadly radiation.

Chapter XXV

NUCLEAR EMERGENCY SEARCH TEAM

In 1983, Glenn was asked to become part of the US Department of Energy's Nuclear Emergency Search Team. This elite Nevada Test Site group was known as "the NEST." Their job was to train our allies on procedures to follow if an emergency nuclear disaster should occur on their land. Glenn was sent to London to help train the British on procedures to follow should a nuclear emergency occur there. He spent two weeks training the Brits, and he developed a long-term friendship with the group he trained.

Glenn was a loyal and dedicated worker for his employer (REECo) and to the AEC. He was liked and admired by all. A folder full of commendation letters, many plaques, mugs, clocks, and much more attest to that fact. He had total trust and faith in the *system* to protect him from overexposure to the deadly radiation he was required to work in on a daily basis. But in reality, unknown to him, he had been dramatically overexposed to such a degree that he died on June 5, 1999, after suffering tremendously with seven different types of cancer, which had clearly been caused by his constant exposure to deadly ionizing radiation. The cancers invaded his windpipe, and he slowly suffocated to death as the masses grew larger and eventually closed his windpipe completely.

He was once interviewed by a reporter from the *Las Vegas Review Journal*, and this WWII-decorated soldier and dedicated NTS worker commented to her, "I think it's a very important task that we're performing. I feel like I'm part of the national security work for the entire country."

The sad part is ... the government knew what was happening to these men and covered it up. REECo knew and kept quiet. It was a dirty little secret that was kept carefully hidden away by the ones responsible for this atrocity. No one ever thought this information would become public knowledge because the AEC had placed the records in a "classified and confidential" category under the guise of national security! They wanted to make sure no one ever knew about this injustice to the dedicated workers at the NTS. However, through the Freedom of Information Act and political pressure, the DOE was forced to release all of Glenn's employment records.

Chapter XXVI

GLENN'S EMPLOYMENT HISTORY

Eight months before his death, Glenn wrote this short employment history.

I was employed by Reynolds Electrical and Engineering Co., Inc., from June 15, 1958 until January 2, 1987. I wish to address the first 15 years of my employment at which time I worked in the tunnels. I worked in the capacity of Miner, Shift Boss, General Foreman, Asst. Superintendent, Superintendent and Project Manager during those 15 years. I was responsible as Leader and Instructor in use of underground oxygen breathing apparatus, specifically the McCaa.

I also was responsible for all the training on the Test Site for personnel who performed re-entries into the tunnels for safety conditions to help with instrumentation and data recovery relative to the nuclear test. We had very little success with radiation containment in the tunnels in the early years from 1958 to about 1968. During that period of time some severe radiation problems existed for the personnel involved in the re-entries.

During this period of time I led the re-entries on numerous events, including: Evans at B tunnel, Feather at B tunnel, Chena at B tunnel, Yuba at B tunnel, Red Hot at G tunnel, Door Mist at Area 16, Mini Mist at E tunnel, Tiny Tot at Area 15, Piledriver at Area 15, Marshmellow at Area 16, Gumdrop at Area 16, and

Double Play at Area 16. None of these shots contained, with the exception of Yuba and Piledriver. Yuba contained to a degree (I will relate to that later).

The first event I had experience with re-entry was Tamalpais in 1958 at B tunnel. When the initial re-entry was made, the re-entry team was advised that there was no radiation problems, no significant problems underground, other than maybe the lack of sufficient oxygen. It didn't take long to find out that was not true. When the re-entry team was in the tunnel, they were utilizing a lit candle to detect insufficient oxygen, which is a normal practice for underground miners, and it created an explosion which only by the grace of God, the men escaped the tunnel. If the railroad track had not been laid through the blast door area, the blast door would have been sealed shut which would have prevented all the workers from being able to exit the tunnel. Subsequent to that event, it became necessary to rehabilitate the entire tunnel complex in order to get off the two following shots, Shasta and Evans.

While we were decontaminating the tunnel and removing the sandbags, etc., from Tamalpais, they had an event on the level above, either at F tunnel, or C tunnel, causing a large boulder to dislodge from above. The boulder landed on the ventilation stack of the fans at B tunnel, rendering the fans inoperative. That ceased operation at the tunnel until it could be repaired. Reynolds Electric management asked me if I would make a trip up to the portal to where the fan was and see if it could be repaired. A rad-safe employee (I forgot his name) and myself went up there. We each had two hour dosimeters and the rad-safe monitor carried a gamma detector. When we got about 150 yards from the portal, the rad-safe monitor said he would stop there. The readings on his redactor at that point was 14R. I told him I could not ascertain whether the fans were operable at that point and I would have to go on up to the portal, which I did. I looked at the fans and after much scrutiny, determined that the housing could not rotate. It took approximately 30 minutes to determine what damage had been done. I have no way of knowing how high the radiation level was at the portal. I do know that the dosimeter which I carried in my pocket pegged out at 2R a long time before I reached the portal. Rad-safe monitor and I went back to staging area and reported to management that we could rehabilitate the fans because only the housing was damaged. If it was straightened then the fans would become operative.

Subsequently, the portal was decontaminated by various means to get the radiation levels down and the fans were repaired. The tunnel was decontaminated to allow re-entry and rehabilitation. Of course, we recognized that 100 MR per hour was considered a safe construction zone during that period of time Hard Tack Phase II Testing Program.

The second event I was involved in was Evans in B04 which was executed in September 1958. It did not contain either. In fact, radiation levels were so high in there that we abandoned the tunnel back in the B04 area.

Chapter XXVII

MORATORIUM

The moratorium on October 1, 1958 created several significant problems. We had to scale down our working people to, more or less, a maintenance level, or you might say, to retain a cadre of professionals who could expand in the event nuclear testing began again.

During the moratorium numerous mining re-entries were made. All of them were very highly radioactive and we got quite a bit of exposure in those areas. We did a mining re-entry into Rainer wherein we excavated the tunnel back to ground zero, then sank a shaft down to the bottom of the cavity. We tried to determine the outline of the cavity and we could see it in various places by the glass that was formed by the nuclear detonation which was black in color, which was highly radioactive. The Ranier shaft that we sank was highly contaminated with Alpha and it was necessary for us to wear respirators when we were mining. However, severe working conditions gave considerable problems in affecting the mining. The temperature was exceeding 110 degrees and the humidity was 80 plus percent all the time. The sweat from working made the mas slip around on your face, causing the mask to leak and you weren't breathing through the respirator.

Secondly, the respirator, because of the moisture, the filters would get plugged which would not allow you to breathe. It was quite an ordeal in sinking the shaft.

Subsequent to this re-entry we all went down to E tunnel which was the only other complex in existence at that time. They wanted to do some mining re-entry on the logan. As we mined back in through the logan area, we encountered seams and stratus that were exceeding 3R radiation and our only means of protecting ourselves from the radiation was by trying to put lead sheeting over these areas. I guess we did a pretty good job—we never did know because no one told us.

Subsequent to the logan re-entry our crew went back to B tunnel. Lawrence Livermore Laboratory (LLL), in conjunction with Sandia, had determined that they wanted to create a sphere at the bottom of a shaft which would be codenamed, "Linen", and would be 5kt high explosive test. While the plans were being made, we spent time dressing down the tunnel. One thing that we encountered was that no one (including rad-safe monitors), knew the amount of radon-thoron radiation.

I was in B tunnel, B02 drift, one afternoon with one of my workers, and a rad-safe monitor, when the rad-safe monitor told us that the radiation from radon-thoron was exceeding 250,000 counts. We were wearing no protective clothing and the rad-safe monitor thought nothing of it. While we were working on the shaft, LLL made a determination that they wanted to re-enter Evans drift, B04. They had a sample back there they had to recover which was gold encased in lead. We set up a mine rescue team to go in and make the recovery. As usual, I led the mine rescue team. However, prior to going in, I talked to the experimenters who had installed this sample. They told me it had a one-eighth tracing cable which I could follow to the canister, and it was locked on with a one-quarter inch nut. They said I could take the cable off, and then be able to remove this canister from a drill hole, and it oy weighed about 25 pounds. We made the re-entry and when I got back to the location of the canister, I found that it was a three-quarter inch cable and the nuts were three-quarter inch, and after finally getting that off, I found that the canister weighed in excess of 100 pounds. As I pulled it out of the hole, it fell with me, cutting my finger. I was able to lift it up and carry it to the main drift. We had an incident with one of the members who had sprained his ankle and they had sent in the rescue team for him with a stretcher. I asked him how he felt and he told me he could walk alright, so we put the sample on the stretcher and carried it out to the portal

One thing we found out much later was that the radiation we were dealing with back in the tunnel, the experimenters called, "bowl", was in truth … tritium, and it was a very high level. None of us were aware of this and we all got a good dose of tritium. LLL had the crew taking three urine samples each week, and they fed us salt tablets to assist in getting rid of the radiation in our system. Sometime after this, rad-safe, in conjunction with the AEC, and others, started giving us a 6 pack of beer to drink after work. They did find out a good thing, that one of the crew members would not drink at all, and it showed the deterioration of the tritium out of his system was about flat line, and the rest of the crew showed a decay rate of about thirty degree angle down the chart. So the beer did a job of getting the tritium out of our system, however, what damage it did while it was in our bodies, no one knows.

That was a major effort we did during the moratorium and when nuclear testing resumed in 1961, we had already started working on an event at B tunnel which was called, "Feather". At E tunnel, they would be doing an event which was called "Antler". Antler was the first one executed and I was on the back-up re-entry team. As they neared the re-entry team neared the portal, they had a secondary explosion that blew out the portal. We never did find out the cause. The rad-safe monitor reported on the net that the water in the drainage pond, just off the dump at E tunnel, right next to the highway, was reading 72R.

On the Feather event, one thing that was different, we decided to try and maintain our ventilation so that we could turn our fans on, ventilate the tunnel, and get rid of the radiation into the atmosphere, rather than keeping it in the work area. A ventilation duct was laid on the mesa, and a drill hole from the tunnel to the mesa was made. When the event was executed, it was my job to go with two rad-safe men (but Security would only allow me to have one), to go to the mesa and ascertain if the ventilation system was functional. We got up there and the ground motion from the event had broken the ventilation pipe at many seams and it was rendered useless. So the rad-safe monitor told me to make my analysis of what I had to do and he would do more checking elsewhere. It stated it was pretty safe because it was only reading a few R, and the wind was blowing away from us. The rad-safe monitor left, and while he was gone, the wind changed direction and was coming right over the ventilation pipe towards me, which I was unaware of at the time. When the rad-safe monitor came back, he made a report on the net to control located below, and as soon as he told them the radiation levels, which were extremely high, they insisted they get me off the mesa immediately because I had already exceeded my yearly dose at that time, and I was working on a waiver then. It was suggested by a rad-safe supervisor that I 'lose' my film badge, which I did. We miners were always in fear of losing our jobs if we got too much radiation and could not work.

Our next event was at B tunnel was, "Chena", in 1962. At that time I had more radiation already than my waiver would permit. I had been on a waiver in 1961 and also in 1962. I was in charge of the operation so I had to do all of my work at the portal, through a secondary person. I used one of the LLL employees to take my information to the underground shift boss.

Chena was also an event which did not contain and gave us many radiation problems. The re-entry which I could not work on because of having too much radiation, was a slow, torturous process to get back to the tunnel and not much data was recovered because the underground area was contaminated.

In 1963, we started another event in B tunnel called, "Yuba". Yuba was a different configuration for an event with more thought given to containment. It is difficult to explain the shape of the tunnel, but essentially it was two parallel drifts, sixty feet apart, going back to a cross-cut drift at the end where the device was placed. In the right parallel drifts we left about 30 to 50 feet of solid rock as a pillar between that and the working point. In that pillar the experimenters imbedded cameras which would be recovered upon re-entry. The shot essentially contained, until we went back into the parallel drifts to do the recovery. When we started mining back through the right parallel drift pillar, we found that the drill hole where the power cables to the cameras had been placed, instead of being grouted full, were just plugged with a small amount of putty, which did not seal. We didn't recognize there was a hazard beyond this so all of us got an extreme dose, again, of tritium. In fact, several of the employees had to be sent to Donner Laboratory to get a full body count analysis.

Subsequent to that, all mining that we had to perform, that is excavating the 50 foot tunnel, had to be performed under air supplied equipment. This consisted of a full face mask, with a long hose that was attached to a regulator, which was fed by bottled air. The only problem we encountered there was in moving back and forth between tasks that seemed to occur, the miners were always tangling our hoses together so eventually we could not move until we stopped to straighten them out. However, we did mine out the tunnel in a very short period of time. We were able to recover the cameras, some in reasonable condition, others were damaged. I do not know the results of the reports from that test.

After that period, I moved to Area 15 to take over an operation called, "Piledriver". At this point in time, LLL had basically left the tunnels and gone to the flatlands for their testing in drill holes. DNA did the tunnel events from that point on essentially. They did have LASL and LLL provided the devices so they had to be participants in the events. DNA did much more work to contain the tests and from test to test, the success rate improved dramatically.

Piledriver was executed June 6, 1966. It did contain, however, it completely tore up the access shaft to the collar. It upheaved the ground at the surface, 12 feet back around ground zero, which was 1,500 feet from the shaft collar. It did a lot of surface spall. We did mine back down into Piledriver and re-entered all the test drifts to ascertain the survival of the different configurations of hardening that we had done.

During Piledriver we started a project called, "Tiny Tot", which was a cavity experiment. This was about 60 feet across and 135 feet high, tilted on a 34 degree angle. It was to simulate a surface detonation on the ground. It pretty well contained and we mined back in, through the stemming area, looked at the cavity area, and everything was still intact for the most part. It was considered a successful event.

During the time frame from 1963 through 1968 or 1969, I led re-entries in Area 16, which were the following events: Marshmellow, Gumdrop, and Tiny Tot in Area 15. I participated in the re-entry at Midi Mist at E tunnel. I led the re-entry at Door Mist in Area 16. These events pretty much contained, however, they all had radiation leakage at some point.

One of our main problems with radiation leakage was through the cables. Eventually, gas blocking was installed in the cables which precluded this, but at the outset, we had a lot of leakage of high radiation levels coming through the cables themselves.

I spent my time through 1970 at the tunnels, making re-entries, driving tunnels, and managing tunnels. In 1971, I was promoted to Department Manager and went to Area 3 to take over the Los Alamos Laboratory level of construction effort.

One thing of note—from the period of 1958 through 1968, we had no formal guidelines to make re-entries. In 1968, Sandia Laboratory published a manual titled, "General Tunnel Re-Entry Procedures for Department of Defense, Sandia Laboratory Nuclear Tests". I am enclosing a copy of this publication. As you can see, even with these guidelines, we were still permitted to go into highly hazardous areas.

Also, over a two year period, in preparation for, and removal after the tunnel events, I had excessive exposure to ground up asbestos. We placed the asbestos, by hand, with no breathing protection.

—Glenn A. Clayton

Chapter XXVIII

RADIATION EXPOSURE HISTORY

In the DOE declassified records, which totaled 1,370 pages, of special interest was Glenn's "DOE radiation exposure history." The discrepancies and cover-ups in those records is criminal. Among those pages are missing radiation exposure cards. Those cards were required on a monthly basis. When the workers were in an especially hazardous area, radiation exposure was checked on a daily basis. Missing radiation exposure cards broke all rules. Because of Glenn's unique background in mining, from the very beginning of his employment at the NTS, the radiation cover-ups began to keep him in that position. He was constantly called on to do things no other employee was qualified to do.

The DOE radiation exposure history was a government form that was used to record radiation contamination exposure to employees in mrem's. MREM is defined as "a unit of effective absorbed dose of ionizing radiation in human tissue."

Information listed on the "evaluation of Clayton records" report begins in 1958 and shows, "Film badge readings show gamma radiation exposure to be 2,680mrem. Nasal swipe test shows radiation contamination. This accumulate radiation exposure does not show on the DOE Radiation Exposure History." (That is possibly the very beginning of the deliberate cover-up.)

In the previously classified records released, there were also thirty pages of documents that were number-coded and could only be read with a code book. Those records are still a mystery because the DOE has continually refused access to the actual code book.

More evidence of a cover-up came when the DOE was asked to produce the MTL (material testing laboratory) documents, a very important part of the information obtained after a nuclear blast. They responded to this request by saying, "Those records were kept in one of the tunnels and were so contaminated that we had to bury them so no one would be harmed."

A 1959 memo dated September 4, 1959, from REECo to the AEC states:

"It is requested that the individual listed below be authorized to receive a cumulative occupational radiation exposure of up to 12,000mrem per calendar year. This request is made in accordance with SOP-NTO-0302-044(c)." The name listed *below* was none other than Glenn A. Clayton. In October, his radiation exposure was already at 11,900, and by the end of that year, he had exceeded the 12,000mrem annual limit by several mrems.

Then just a few weeks later on October 13, 1959, the following memo was sent to Glenn's area manager from the radiation safety chief:

"It would be my recommendation that Mr. Clayton be transferred from his present work assignment, to an area where his radiation exposure possibilities would be removed entirely." That didn't happen. Urine samples taken from October 1959 show contamination in November and December; however, this dosage is *not* included in the DOE radiation exposure history.

In 1960, only film badges accounted for the entire year. AEC standard operating procedures, NTSO-0524 in particular, states "Film badges will be attached and worn with security badge and will be exchanged *every month*." No exceptions!

The DOE office refused to get copies of Glenn's missing film badge cards, instead saying, "There is no cost effective way to get the missing film badge cards."

In 1962, on several different occasions, Glenn gave urine samples that the lab was supposed to test for contamination by tritium, gross fission product, uranium, and plutonium. On the three-lined pages that were supposed to show the results of these tests, the remarks section notes at least seventy times, "Not enough for test" or "spilled sample." No *remarks* were listed on the other lines. They were all left blank. So it stands to reason that if the tests were actually done, the results were hidden or destroyed. If the tests were not done, the contamination he might have received went unaccounted for. Either way, Glenn was the loser.

On June 5, 1963, during the Yuba incident, the problem was an overexposure to iodine. A Rad-Safe monitor logbook stated, "Workers complained of nausea. Thyroid readings on employees increased. Lead shielding was used for protection. Iodine was a big problem."

The film badge cards were missing for Glenn from June 7, 1963, to July 29, 1963. Guess what occurred in that time period?

A film badge card from May 2, 1964, shows Glenn had 5,675mrem of radiation exposure. The DOE radiation exposure history shows *zero* radiation exposure.

Listed on the database report, it shows different names used to record Glenn's radiation exposure, which is clearly against the rules. That exposure was listed under four different names—Glenn Aaron Clayton, Glen A. Clayton, Glenn A. Clayton, and Clayton.

A film badge card dated February 2, 1965, shows 6,276mrem exposure for that year. A film badge card dated April 1, 1965, shows 6,488mrem exposure for that year too. The entire DOE radiation exposure history for those two months shows 265mrem this year.

Another film badge card shows contamination to deadly plutonium (239Pu). The DOE radiation exposure history states the dosage was so low it wasn't counted. Scientific reports on plutonium indicate that just one speck of plutonium breathed into your lungs cannot be removed and *will* cause your death as a result of cancer in your lungs. The pattern of radiation exposure denial by the DOE continued through 1970.

History of Glenn's Cancers

- 1992—Small cell bronchogenic carcinoma, left lung (chemo and radiation)
- 1992— Pituitary tumor resection (transsphonoidal craniotomy)
- 1994—Melanoma of the posterior neck (surgically removed)
- 1995—Melanoma of the ear (surgically removed and grafted)
- 1995—High-grade transitional cell carcinosarcoma (removed bladder)
- 1997—Pituitary macroadenoma (right pterional craniotomy of the pituitary)
- 1998—Squamous cell carcinoma with necrosis, left lung (chemotherapy)
- 1999—Died July 5, 1999. Cancers invaded windpipe, closing off air supply.

PRIVACY ACT MATERIAL REMOVED

Personnel Radiation Exposures	September 4, 1959
	NTS-3246-R

Mr. W. W. Allaire
Director

Nevada Operations Division
U. S. Atomic Energy Commission
Albuquerque Operations Office
P. O. Box 5400
Albuquerque, New Mexico

Gentlemen:

It is requested that the individuals listed below be authorized to receive a cumulative occupational radiation exposure of up to 10 rem per person for the current calendar year. This request is made in accordance with SOP-NTO-0502-044(c).

Name	Annual Exposure (rem)		Age (years)
	-5°	15.°°	
Clayton, Glenn A.	2.000	8.300	35

PRIVACY ACT MATERIAL REMOVED

* Exposure to date summated with internal exposure extrapolated to infinity.
** Extension to 8 rem for employee only due to his age.

All persons listed are presently employed by REECo and all their total occupational radiation history has been accumulated with REECo. For this reason there is no occupational exposure earlier than shown by the above tabulation. These facts are documented in our dosimetry records.

PRIVACY ACT MATERIAL REMOVED

PRIVACY ACT MATER. REMOVED

October 13, 19—

James R. Crockett　　　　　　　　　　　　William S. Johnson

Personnel Radiation Exposures

　　　　The following is a list of significant radiation exposures which have been accumulated this year through September for the individuals shown. It is recommended that the appropriate supervision be provided with this information to guide their future actions when work in radiation areas is involved.

　　　　While nobody can give complete assurance that these people will not exceed the permissible level of 12 rem for 1959, our exposure history for September indicates that the work areas are well controlled. Except in the case of Glen Clayton, there is enough left in the bank to cover these employees short of some untoward incident. It would be my recommendation that Mr. Clayton be transferred from his present work assignment to an area where his exposure possibilities would be removed entirely.

Name	Organization Number	Accumulated Dose (Rem) External and Internal 1959 to Date (10/1/59)
Clayton, G.	57-07	

PRIVACY ACT MATER. REMOVED

ORIGINAL SIGNED BY
WILLIAM S. JOHNSON

William S. Johnson

Chapter XXIX

OTHER SECRETS

One of Glenn's jobs, which was never mentioned in any of the records, included building a road to a special location in Area 51, which was located adjacent to the NTS. All details were confidential, and they've remained classified, as Area 51 is still a super-secret facility today.

Area 51 was established in April 1955 by the CIA for Project Aquatone. This project was used for the development of the Lockheed U-2 strategic reconnaissance aircraft, which was also known as the "U-2 spy plane."

Most likely that was the only NTS job assigned to Glenn where he was not exposed to some type of deadly radiation!

One of the workers at NTS was responsible for retaining all records for the NTS workers—records that detailed toxic materials reports, personnel rosters, weekly safety meetings, accident logbooks, and lists of miners and craftsmen who reentered a tunnel where nuclear bomb tests were conducted. These employee records were kept in cardboard boxes in a hundred green and white Xerox boxes. These boxes held all employee records from 1970 to 1995 and were stored in a building at the entrance to N Tunnel in Area 12. It was not an easy job to accomplish, but the worker was diligent and thorough. The worker went back to the building in 1998 to check on the records, but someone had removed them. It was later revealed that the hundred boxes of important employee records were picked up by a forklift operator who carted them off to a landfill at the NTS where they were buried.

We should also note how many times the name of the government agency representing the NTS has changed. In the beginning it was called the "Atomic Energy Commission" (AEC). Then in 1975, it became "Energy Research and Development Administration" (ERDA). In 1977, ERDA ceased operation, and the Department of Energy (DOE) was founded on August 4, 1977.

The DOE then assumed responsibility of overseeing the Nevada Test Site operation. Even with the name changes, however, the discrepancies in reporting radiation exposure to the employees continued. Every time the name changed, that meant discarding letterhead stationery, forms, among other items and replacing them with things that had the new agency's name on everything. Money was no object!

In 1974, one of the subcontractors was required to close their Las Vegas office and move everything from the Las Vegas office to the Nevada Test Site. Almost 150 employee jobs were eliminated, and office supplies for engineers, draftsmen, and office staff were discarded in the trash dumpster in back of the Las Vegas office. As a reason for discarding the materials, they said, "Because it would cost more to return those office supplies to General Service Administration than they are worth." The GSA was the supplier of all government office supplies, equipment, and forms. Some of the employees asked if they could take some of the reams of paper, drafting pens, engineering forms, and anything they could use. The answer they got was a loud *no!* They were told, "If you take anything considered belonging to the government, even if it is taken from the trash dumpster, and you are caught with that property in your possession, that equates to a theft from the federal government! That is a federal offense, and you will spend some time in jail."

The Nevada Test Site had many different areas that were closely monitored for radiation exposure and aftereffects of nuclear blasts. For instance, in Area 2, you could see three typical American houses built to scale, and through the windows you could see four manikins (man, woman, and two children) sitting at a table. The results of contamination and the damage done by a nuclear blast were never reported. Houses and manikins seemed to remain intact.

In Area 15, there was a horse farm and a dairy farm complete with cows and a bull. Cowboys were hired to take care of the livestock in this area. The cow's milk was tested frequently for contamination. The scientists had a type of see-through oval-shaped glass (or plastic) contraption inserted into the side of the cow's stomach so they could observe what was happening in the stomach area. The information gathered from this *experiment* was never released.

Chapter XXX

SOLDIERS IN FOXHOLES

In the mid-1950s, a group of Army soldiers were taken to the NTS and told to dig a foxhole where they could all "relax and enjoy the greatest show on earth!"

As the soldiers were clustered in foxholes five feet deep, they watched the Cold War explode in front of their eyes. A commanding officer would bark out, "The explosion will sound like you are standing near the muzzle of a tremendous artillery piece as it is fired. Then you will hear rocks and debris flying past your heads. Stay in your trench!" The soldiers obeyed every word their commanding officer said. One of the soldiers later reported that after the rocks and debris stopped falling, the soldiers looked out from their foxholes and observed the biggest mushroom cloud they had ever seen.

Tourists visiting Las Vegas, a tiny gambling town at that time, were warned by a single red-and-blue light on Main Street when a nuclear blast was to occur. Unleashing weapons ranging up to sixty-five thousand times as powerful as those dropped on Hiroshima and Nagasaki, scientists at the Nevada Test Site have played a pivotal role in the nuclear arms race.

Chapter XXXI

THE REST OF THE STORY

Almost right away, a very puzzling part of this NTS story began to unfold. The Nevada elected officials, with their Washington connections, began making noises about paying the widows of those deceased Nevada Test Site workers. Puzzling to say the least, because their role had always been to sweep that sort of thing under the nearest rug. It was obvious that some recent changes had occurred. It was around this time that President Clinton showed an interest in this 'situation'. His Department of Energy at the Nevada Test Site had, for years, covered up their dirty little secrets about thousands of men dying from radiation induced cancers caused from working in the Area 12 tunnels where nuclear bombs had been detonated. The local administrators had simply been doing what they had always done when families tried to get their hands on records which might support a claim or lawsuit. Families were told that those employment records were 'classified government property' and not to be released to anyone. The DOE had been doing business as usual, and exactly in the manner they had been instructed, for years.

As a result of the press conference our Nevada Senator held in my home, bits of information began to trickle out. People saw the press conference on TV and read the account in the Las Vegas newspaper. The agencies involved in the NTS cover-up of radiation exposure to the workers, could no longer deny their involvement. So, the DOE stated they wanted to 'right a wrong' which had been going on for years. Now, we all know that politicians never do what they do simply because it's the right and honorable thing to do. So why would the DOE, all of a sudden want to do the right thing? That was a question that needed to be answered.

This was an election year and the party in power would stand to gain many votes if they could get a compensation program approved by election time. A little cadre was set up by the Department of Labor to pay claims. They started out with a lot of publicity in the Nevada media (which was already controlled by them), so the party in power could reap a harvest of good will, votes and contributions. The whole thing paid off, and the same politicians were re-elected.

The next hurdle was to figure out how much one life was worth, and how much one dying man suffering from deadly radiation cancers is worth. The only way to get that information, and make any type of determination on compensation, was to have access to an employee's radiation exposure records. All eyes suddenly turned to the 1,370 pages of declassified employment records on Glenn Clayton. Although, they recognized that Glenn's radiation exposure was 'off the charts', the DOE did not want to admit that a lot of the other employees, working in the same areas, suffered from the same deadly radiation exposure. Problem was that their radiation exposure records showed a much lower radiation exposure than Glenn. No one could answer the question as to 'how' that was possible?

Now we all know that the government never wants to give away money, they only want to take your money. And so, the question as to who was going to get paid became a 'hot issue'. In order to have a 'fair' compensation program, the DOL established the following guidelines:

   a. It was to be for government employees only.
   b. It covered only certain employees.
   c. It covered only selected locations.
   d. It did not cover the contractors at the NTS.
   e. It covered only certain types of cancers.
   f. It appeared not to cover the majority of cancers caused by exposure to deadly nuclear radiation, ever present, in the Area 12 tunnels.

In this "fair" government compensation program, many employees were disqualified in the selection process. And, very few potential recipients were notified that they were even eligible to apply for compensation.

Research indicated that no one with radiation induced cancer had ever won a lawsuit against the government. This indicates that Uncle Sam doesn't want to pay for losses it causes.

After many months of the DOL 'fine tuning' the compensation program, in 2002, it was ready to be implemented.

The final determination:

1. Only the ones not falling under any of the categories listed above would eligible.
2. Compensation amount would be $150,000.
3. Compensation for workers dying would be: All medical expenses would be covered.

This experience, with all of its troubles and trials, has certainly been an eye opener and certainly worth the effort.

I am thankful for the opportunity of meeting so many wonderful widows and for being able to help them qualify for this compensation program.

The government was finally forced to compensate widows whose husband's radiation exposure records showed far less radiation exposure than Glenn's. A strange thing because those men worked side by side with Glenn in extremely hazardous, deadly radiation filled tunnels, on a daily basis!

6/1/17

To Rabbi,

Thanks you for all you do!

Love,
Matt

ABOUT THE AUTHOR

Dorothy Clayton was born and raised in small town USA. She graduated from Texas High School in Texarkana, Texas and continued her education at Crosier Business College in Dallas, Texas.

In 1961, Dorothy was hired by Bendix Field Engineering to set up office for NASA's Apollo program. After a short stay in Cape Canaveral, Florida, the family moved to Las Vegas, Nevada where she soon found herself working with The Atomic Energy Commission at the Nevada Test Site as part of the Nuclear Weapons Testing Program.

The Cold War was in full swing, and there was a patriotic and winning spirit by everyone working at the NTS. All work was extremely secret and

certainly not discussed with anyone outside the NTS gates. Everyone knew the main task was to contrive "the perfect" weapon, certainly before the Soviet Union accomplished that task.

Dorothy witnessed first hand, the devastation of those tests as workers began dying with all types of cancers.

Little did she know that she would become part of an elite group of Americans know as the Veterans of the Cold War while others became casualties of the Cold War.

CPSIA information can be obtained
at www.ICGtesting.com
Printed in the USA
LVOW11s1228250517
535613LV00004B/564/P

9 781489 710529